Future Geographies

Graham Senior

Acknowledgements

I would like to thank the following people who pledged their support to the original Summer Holiday Textbook Project in August 2021.

Edward Senior, Milnthorpe, Cumbria; Hannah Senior, Coventry, Warwickshire; Caroline Jones, Woking, Surrey; Penny Ivers, Coventry, Warwickshire; Stephanie Miller, Bolton, Lancashire; Matthew Beavan, Leicester, Leicestershire; Tom Paper, San Francisco, California; Cat Gifford, Aberdeen, Aberdeenshire; Helen Nurton; Kate Parry-Jones, Newport, Gwent; Paula Frost, Redhill, Surrey; Georgina Fowler, Castleford, West Yorkshire; Katy Conlon, Rotherham, South Yorkshire; Sarah Black, Ipswich, Suffolk and Phil Thornton, Greater London

Most of the images in the text are sources from pxhere.com. If I have inadvertently used material without obtaining the necessary permissions, please contact me at geogwriter@gmail.com and I will endeavour to make amends.

A note from the author

This is not a textbook about ox-bow lakes, longshore drift, or China's long-abandoned One Child Policy. There are enough of those. Rather it is an introduction to several issues that are going to become increasingly important as we approach the second quarter of the twenty-first century. Here are over thirty topics that students ought to be informed about, ideally before they complete Key Stage Three - and especially the ones that have decided to do GCSE History. There is enough material here for a year's lessons, if supplemented with appropriate documentaries and other suitable content. It is dedicated to all the students who have endured being taught by me and colleagues who have taught alongside me at Fullbrook School, New Haw (1993-2001), Bishop Reindorp School, Guildford (2001-2003), Christ's College, Guildford (2003-2012), Blue Coat School, Coventry (2012-2017) and Nicholas Chamberlaine School, Bedworth (2019-).

Contents

*Eternal Father, strong to save, whose
arm doth bind the restless wave*

*Who bids the mighty ocean deep, its
own appointed limits keep ...*

William Whiting, 1860

Background

Among the more depressing claims made about the future of the planet is that the rate at which sea levels are rising is only going to continue to increase. Scientists estimate that, since the 1880s, mean sea level has increased by 23 centimeters and that almost half of that increase has taken place in the last 25 years. They currently anticipate that sea level will continue to rise by at least 3 mm every year for the foreseeable future. The reasons why sea levels are rising are twofold. First, there is the extra liquid water that is dumped in the oceans as the **glacier**s and ice caps continue to melt, but the sea also expands as it gets warmer. These two factors are equally to blame for the rising sea levels, each accounting for about 50% of the rise. Confusingly, however, the increase in sea level is not the same all over the world. This is because currents in the ocean and the atmosphere mean that water is not evenly distributed, neither is the force of gravity the same everywhere. What is even more bizarre, the extra water that melting ice caps dump in the sea hardly affects sea levels near the poles at all but, instead, makes the oceans deeper near the **equator**.

Why does it matter?

Keeping the sea in its place is important for many reasons. Forty percent of the world's population, which amounts to roughly 3 billion people at present, live within 100 kilometers of the sea. But, if the sea were to continue to rise at its current rate, the **habitat**s of birds, fish and plants would also be lost, **wetland**s would be flooded, and agricultural land become choked with salt. The rate of coastal erosion would also increase. Other effects would include the large-scale migration and/or isolation of coastal communities and damage to coastal **infrastructure** including the roads, cables and pipelines that connect them. Addressing the problem of rising sea levels also matters because they make tropical storms worse. From 1963 until 2012, for example, it is estimated that up to 50% of all the deaths caused by tropical storms were not as a result of high winds, but rather of swollen oceans. It is also significant that a disproportionate number of low-income households and communities of colour are vulnerable to the advance of the sea.

Adaptation and Mitigation

Broadly speaking, there are two approaches to this problem. One type of response is called **mitigation**. This is when we take action to try and limit the effect that sea level rises have on us. The other, adaptation, is when we accept that the changes are going to take place and change our habits and lifestyles accordingly.

Mitigation strategies that have been used include building vast sea walls. This is the case in the city of Jakarta, the capital of Indonesia. Here there are plans to build a wall 80 m high around the entire city which is currently sinking by around 10 cm every year - mainly because its inhabitants are helping themselves to groundwater supplies illegally, causing it to subside. In South Korea, the Saemangeum Seawall was completed in 2010 which, at 33 km would bridge the gap between England and France at its narrowest point. It has also been suggested that low-lying areas could be raised by bringing sand and gravel in from elsewhere or by building islands and breakers out at sea from solid waste to combat coastal erosion. This also has the advantage that, if the waste used to be incinerated, burying it under the sea instead will help to reduce emissions of carbon dioxide.

Supporters of adaptation, on the other hand, take the view that putting up a fight against the sea is futile and that it would be better to learn to live with and even to take advantage of higher sea levels. Those who think this way might suggest that we should learn to live afloat, whether on boats on river **deltas** or in vast floating cities that are not unlike the cruise ships on which many people already enjoy their holidays. They also point out that flooded coastal areas could be used to grow crops that can tolerate salty water, to farm fish or to grow plants to be used as **biofuel**. The latter, however, has the drawback that, when the **biofuels** were burned, they would put back much of the carbon dioxide that they absorbed while growing. There is even the suggestion that low-lying, poor-quality housing at the water's edge should be replaced with multi-story apartments whose lowest levels would not be used for living on, but rather as stations for a public water taxi service like the ones that operate in places like Amsterdam, Bangkok, London and Tokyo.

1.

   a. From the data provided in the text, make your own predictions about the rate at which sea levels might continue to rise.

   b. What do you think is the (i) worst-case scenario; (ii) best-case scenario and (iii) most realistic scenario?

2.

   a. Which countries stand to lose the most in the event of large-scale sea-level rise?

   b. Do you think that they should (i) put up a fight against the advancing waves or (ii) accept that sea-level rise is inevitable and change their way of life accordingly?

3. Would you consider a life afloat? What would appeal to you and/or put you off the idea?

Background

It is now over thirty years since the threat of a warmer world first became front-page news. Since then, the conversation has largely changed from "When is it going to happen?" to "How bad is it going to get?". Some people suggest that limiting the overall increase in temperature to +3°C during the current century is still a possibility if countries work together on low-carbon technologies. However, others think that this is a lost cause with some modelers even predicting that, if countries carry on maximising their use of fossil fuels in a bid to get richer and richer, the increase could be more like +5°C, or even worse.

It's getting hot out there

Few people think that **global warming** this is still something that can be ignored. In northwest USA in 2021, for example, 62 people died in the state of Oregon in a single month from heat-related illness while, in 2003, sustained temperatures over 40°C across France killed 15,000 people. It is being suggested that, rather than taking place once every 3-5 years, heatwaves will soon occur at least twice every year. They will also be more keenly felt in towns and cities where the temperature can be significantly warmer as buildings and people act like huge storage radiators. A warmer world will also be a less productive one. Crop yields could be reduced by up to 30% across the whole world by 2050, with the greatest reduction being seen in tropical and subtropical areas. People will also be less productive as high temperatures and high humidity sap their energy. Rising temperatures are also likely to affect us mentally with psychologists arguing that, if we do not act, we are likely to be overcome by feelings of both guilt and helplessness. "We don't know what the future is going to look like", said one, adding that we might end up feeling fearful and start blaming ourselves for the situation. Another commentator pointed out that, in a hotter world, there would be fewer resources so people and countries will become increasingly wary of one another.

What can be done?

The response to rising global temperatures needs to take place at an individual level and a societal one. In the short term, individuals can protect themselves from extreme heat by staying indoors and staying hydrated. They can alter their work patterns; as has long been the case in Spain where everyone rests during that part of the day when the sun is at its height; and limit physical activity to the early morning or late evening. They also need to be educated about how to cope with the extreme heat as the best course of action is not always the most obvious. This is shown in the example of Chicago in 1995, when it was common to board up your windows in order not to become a victim of crime. But when elderly people started using fans to alleviate the heat in their boarded-up homes, they turned them into **convection** ovens and literally roasted themselves. France has also introduced a heatwave warning system that monitors various critical indicators of an impending crisis. This can alert carers to check up on vulnerable adults. Nearly everyone living in a warmer climate is likely to need universal air conditioning by 2100 and this need to be budgeted for, not only in terms of how much money it will cost but also in terms of how much stress it will put on energy resources.

In the longer term, there are other possibilities. First, we must look to better management of the world's water supplies, particularly to harvesting and storing the storm waters that will rise as rainfall becomes more intense. We also need to continue to do research into heat-resistant crops such as wheat and maize, staple foods that can survive periods of heat stress. Planting trees, particularly in urban areas (known as urban forestry), will slow down rates of **infiltration**, while also increasing **transpiration** which will help to drive city temperatures down. Added to this, trees also provide somewhere to sit in the shade and avoid the intense midday sun. Then there is the idea of the green roof which involves planting the spaces on the tops of tall buildings with grass and trees. This fulfils some of the same functions and can both intercept heavy rainfall and moderate the warming effect of **urban heat island**s by up to 2-3°C. The prize for the most extreme solution, however, must go to the settlement of Newtok in Alaska. On the shores of the Bering Sea, Newtok was getting over 20 m nearer to the water every year. This alarming rate of coastal erosion was brought about as rising temperatures made the sea expand and brought ever more violent storms ashore. The answer? Choose a new site for your settlement over 15 km inland and move everyone there, lock stock and barrel.

1. This graph, which is taken from the website NOAA Climate.gov | science & information for a climate-smart nation shows how the global average temperature has changed from 1870 until 2020

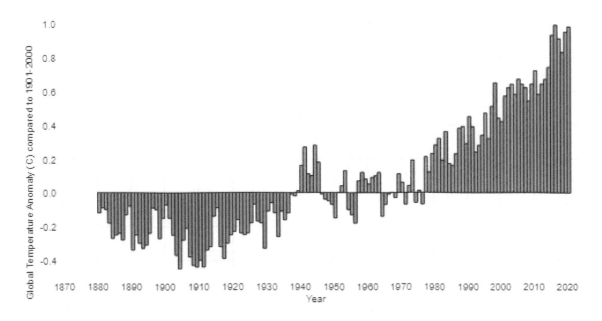

2.

    a. What pattern is clearly visible from the graph?

    b. What reasons other than human activity are offered to explain this? You may need to do some further research.

3. To what extent is the action/inaction of people responsible for the deaths of those who die from a heat-related illness?

4. What else can individuals do to limit the effect of rising temperatures on their own lives?

Background

Bugs, creepy crawlies, critters. From the names that we give many of the insects that we encounter, it's clear that we don't much like them. After all, they sting us, they carry disease, and they ruin our picnics. Without them, there would be no malaria, no insect bites, and no need to use hundreds of thousands of tonnes of **pesticides** on our crops. I could also write this book in peace without being divebombed by flies all day long. So, why don't we just get rid of them, or at least reduce their numbers? After all, there are a million ants for every person on the planet. Who needs this many insects?

We need bugs

Surprisingly, the insects that cause us problems are very much in the minority. We need the many millions of species that do us no harm to work for us. We need them for pollinating the food we eat, breaking down dead matter so that nutrients can be recycled,

giving us wax, silk, and honey, and providing food for animals further up the **food chain.**

Pollen is a fine yellow powder that flowering plants produce to fertilise other plants of the same species. Sometimes it is carried by the wind, but insects do most of the work transferring it from plant to plant. If people had to be employed to do it instead, the annual wage bill could top £200 billion every year. Flowering plants make up 50-90% of a typical human diet as well as a large part of the diets of the animals that we eat. 80% of all plants need pollinating. Without the help of insects there simply would not be enough calories to go around. Insects also pollinate plants that have other uses. Cotton, and flax which is used to make linen, both need insects to do this. Without them, there would be less natural fabric available and the demand for **synthetic fibres** such as polyester would rise, fueling an even greater demand for oil.

We also need insects to help us recycling, not of plastic bottles or cardboard but of dead organic matter. While we probably don't like to think about it too much, flies are the refuse collectors of the natural world. They lay their eggs in piles of dung, in plant and animal waste and in dead animal carcasses so that, when the maggots hatch, they have a ready-made feast to tuck into. Without them, we would eventually disappear under a pile of (very) slowly rotting plants and corpses. Some insects also provide us with raw materials. Honey, for example, has been shown to have several important health benefits, and wax is used to make candles and cosmetics. Silk, meanwhile, is used to make luxurious fabrics. Lastly, insects are an important source of protein for animals higher up the **food chain.** A swallow, for example, needs to be fed 200,000 insects to make it to adulthood.

Where have all the bugs gone?

The decline in the number and variety of insects over recent years has been nothing short of alarming. Some experts predict that we could see as many as 40% of insect species wiped out before 2060. Of particular concern is the decline in the number of moths, butterflies, dung beetles, ants, and bees. What is more, while we can make an educated guess as to why this is happening, there is not enough monitoring going on to get an accurate picture. Many of the problems are a result of intensive agricultural practices, which is when we make the land work too hard to maximise yields. 3 million tonnes of **pesticides** are dumped on the land every year globally, causing water pollution. Meadows, marshland, heaths, and rainforest are also being wiped out, leaving many insects without an appropriate **habitat.**

Being bug-friendly

There are many things that can be done to encourage the insect population. As consumers, we can increase the demand for organic produce, that is food that is produced without the use of **fertilisers** and **pesticides**. It is expensive, but the absence of additives and preservatives in our food has considerable health benefits for us, too, one of which is that we are unlikely to need to use antibiotics so frequently. It would also help to stimulate the agricultural sector and create more jobs on the land.

We can also play a small part to encourage **biodiversity** in our own homes and communities. Planting certain kinds of plants, including buddleia, lavender and chives will help to support a healthy insect population, as will allowing for some 'wild' space in our gardens, where piles of logs, natural ponds and hedges all provide a safe space for a thriving insect community. Education is also the key to success here. People must be taught to value the natural world, not just for what it provides for us but for its own sake. We need to be reminded of the connection between the way in which we treat the land and the quality of the food that it produces for us. Living museums and urban farms can help to achieve this for the many people who rarely venture beyond the suburbs of their own towns and cities.

1. "Insects are just a nuisance." How would you argue against this point of view?

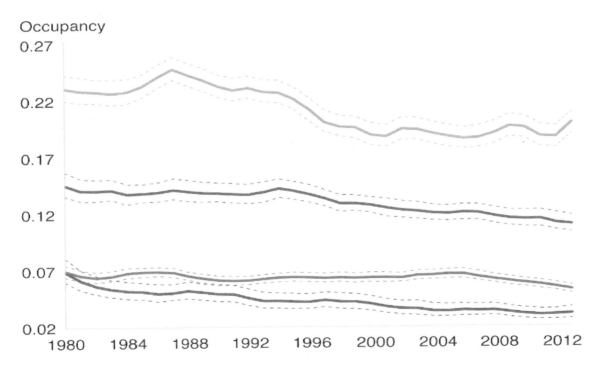

Decline in pollinating insects in Britain

═══ Widespread species of wild bee and hoverflies
━━━ Widespread southern species of wild bees and hoverflies
━━━ Wild bees and hoverflies living in southern areas
━━━ Wild bees and hoverflies living in upland areas

Occupancy

Occupancy is an estimate of the proportion of 1km grid cells where the species is present

Source: Nature Communications

BBC

2. Why is the number and variety of insects in decline?

3. This chart shows the decline in various species of pollinating insects in the UK

   a. Describe the trends that you can see

   b. Why does it matter if the UK's bee population is in decline?

4. What could you do to encourage insects to visit your garden, or a local park if you do not have a garden?

Background

The percentage of the earth's surface that is habitable is less than you might think. To begin with, there are the oceans that cover roughly two-thirds of the Earth; so, unless underwater cities are part of your plan, that only leaves one-third. Of what remains, roughly a quarter of the land is too remote or mountainous, making it almost impossible to live there. However, when it comes to the desert, which accounts for one-third of all the dry land, it is a different story. Large areas of the hot deserts, in particular, could be put to better use through desert greening, which is the reclamation of the desert for **biodiversity**, farming and forestry.

Why take action?

We urgently need to stop land on the fringes of hot deserts from becoming useless to people when it comes to farming crops, keeping livestock, and growing trees for firewood.

Already the spread of the desert has affected a quarter of a billion people and it is anticipated that as many as 135 million people will have had to move away from the places where they currently live by 2045 because the land will no longer support them. Soil that can hold neither moisture nor nutrients is also **infertile** and blows around in violent desert storms, blocking roads and railway tracks, burying fences, and covering land which would otherwise be useful.

Whose fault is it?

There are two main causes of **desertification**, natural and manmade. The Earth's temperature is changing all the time, quite apart from anything we might be doing as people to make the situation worse. This is because the sun's output is not constant and because the Earth is not always the same distance from our nearest star. This, in turn, shifts the air and ocean currents around so that it doesn't always rain in the same place. High temperatures also cause high rates of **evaporation** so that, after a time, the ground is covered with a salty crust.

People, however, are making the situation far worse and many find themselves trapped in a spiral of decline. As populations grow, for example in countries on the fringes of the Sahara Desert, people are forced to use the land more intensively. With more mouths to feed, they plant more seeds and keep more animals in the same area year after year. This means that every year they are expecting the land to feed more people and animals than it ever did before. Animals that once just ate the blades of grass that grew, now eat the crops right down to their roots, too, so they cannot regrow. And just like you would, if you were made to work without getting any rest at all, the land gets exhausted and becomes less productive until, eventually, nothing that is planted there grows. Then, when there is nothing to eat and the last tree has been chopped down for firewood, it is no longer possible for people to live there.

What can be done?

There are several ways in which we can stop land on the fringes of the desert from becoming degraded and useless, but they all begin with conserving what little water falls there. A place can receive as much as 249mm of rain a year and still be called a desert. The trouble is that it tends to fall in a few torrential downpours and, within a short space of time, what little rain that does fall has all been lost to run-off or **evaporation** due to the high temperatures. One way to conserve rainwater is by building covered cisterns that prevent it from evaporating in the heat. There is then the matter of distributing the water that has been collected. This can be achieved, if somewhat inefficiently, using canals and aqueducts.

Earthen pipes are a better solution and underground systems are even better than that.

Another way of increasing the water supply is with **desalination** plants, which take the salt out of seawater so that it can be used for cooking and drinking. Stone walls can also be built. These act as a windbreak to stop fragile soils from being blown or washed away. Furthermore, terracing, which involves breaking slopes up into many level steps, also helps to retain moisture and goodness in the soil. This makes it more likely that crops will grow successfully. Crop rotation can also be used to balance the nutrients in the soil, while crops can be covered with plastic sheeting to retain moisture and prevent soil erosion.

What about trees?

When it comes to conserving water and protecting the soil from further damage, however, trees are in a class of their own. Admittedly, they take some time to grow from tiny seedlings into fully grown specimens, but once this is achieved the benefits are enormous. Trees store water in their roots and branches; they draw water up from **aquifers** (rocks that contain water) deep below the ground and, by holding the soil together, their roots inhibit erosion. They cool the soil down by providing shade which also reduces **evaporation**. They also attract animals whose droppings and, ultimately, dead bodies increase the organic content of the soil and make it more likely that things will grow in the future.

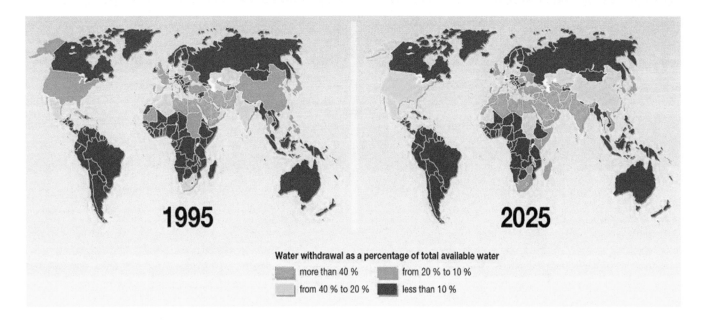

1. This chart shows how the amount of water we are taking out of our rivers, lakes and streams is increasing over time.

    a. Describe the changes that are predicted.

    b. In which countries is the percentage of water withdrawn likely to increase the most?

    c. Why do you think they are likely to need so much water in the future?

2. "In the 20th-century, world water use has grown twice as fast as world population." Steven Solomon. What challenges does this present us with?

3. Could you use less water?

    a. Keep a diary of how much water you use in a typical day. Remember to include direct use (i.e., washing, drinking, showering) and indirect use (i.e. doing the laundry).

    b. Compare your findings with the data found at https://www.ccwater.org.uk/households/using-water-wisely/averagewateruse/.

    c. How does your use of water compare?

Background

If there is one area in which we are failing spectacularly to achieve the kinds of standards, we need to meet to save the planet it is **carbon emissions**. If we are to limit the increase in the average global temperature to no more than +2°C before 2050 then we must get the average amount of CO_2 that each person produces down to one tonne per person per year in under 30 years. The trouble is that even the average UK citizen living in a semi-detached house who uses an average amount of electricity, who drives a modest car around 6,000 miles a year and whose diet includes meat has already clocked up six tonnes - and that is without any foreign holidays, very little processed food, and good recycling habits.

What is a carbon budget, then?

We can calculate a **carbon budget** for a country or an individual by adding together the combined emissions given off by housing, travel, food, and products and services. The USA, for example, was responsible for around 5.0 billion tonnes of emissions in 2016, or 15 tonnes per person. In the UK, it is more like 0.4 billion tonnes, which equates to about 5.5 tonnes per head. However, for many countries in Africa and even some in Asia, the figure is below one tonne per person, which also happens to be the global target for 2050. It's a tough target, by anyone's standards.

What is the scale of change that we need?

It will do little good to tinker around at the edges of your lifestyle if you are going to reduce your **carbon footprint** significantly. Unplugging your phone charger, not leaving appliances on standby, defrosting your fridge and only boiling as much water as you need are all excellent ideas but won't make a lot of difference. We must tackle the high tariff items, such as what you eat, how high you set the thermostat, how you get around, how far and how often you travel abroad and the number of products and services that you consume. An ambitious, yet achievable, target might be to aim for a 'four-tonne lifestyle', one that produced four tonnes of CO_2 per person per year. This chart shows what this would entitle everyone to along with some examples of current practice around the world for comparison.

	To achieve a 'four-tonne lifestyle'	Examples of current habits
Food	A vegan diet with minimal waste	73% of the world's population eat meat and throw away up to one-third of what they buy
Electricity	1,500kWh / year	The typical UK home consumes 3,371 kWh/year
Travel	Around 2,000 miles in a private vehicle/year	Average US citizen already drives over 1,000 miles a month; around 13,500 miles/year
Products and Services	$3,000 per year spent on goods other than food, and services	The author ordered over 100 items on Amazon in six months alone last year!

A 'one-tonne lifestyle' would be even more restrictive and would involve harnessing all the available **low-carbon technology** to meet our needs. Most of that single tonne would have to be allocated to providing food, all electricity, heating, and cooling would have to be from low-carbon sources, and we would not be able to travel to any great extent at all. Journeys would have to be mainly on foot, by bicycle or on electrified public transport such as trams.

A further problem is that we cannot expect everyone in the world to reduce their emissions equally. This is because high-income countries (HICs) have already had their bite of the cherry, already have large footprints, and have the money and technology to reduce their carbon emissions. LICs, on the other hand, must be allowed to increase their **carbon budgets** in the short term so that they can invest in things that will improve their quality of life.

What can we do in the meantime?

Two things that can be done while we wait for better technology to arrive that will reduce our **carbon emissions** are carbon tracking and carbon offsetting. There are many apps that allow you to calculate your current **carbon footprint** by asking questions about where you get your electricity from, what fuel you rely on for heating, how far you travel and by what means and about the kind of diet that you have. Then, when you know the extent of your carbon debt, you can pay it off by investing in projects that promote **sustainability**. To pay my annual 'debt' of six tonnes, for example, I could contribute $90 (about £65) to a project in Malawi that develops fuel-efficient stoves and, in so doing, reduces the demand for firewood. Alternatively, I could donate $45 (about £32) to a hydro-electric project or pay £80 to plant six trees in the UK, each of which, when fully grown, would offset one tonne of emissions.

Hostility

The obstacles to achieving much lower **carbon emissions** are considerable. Quite apart from getting people to radically change their lifestyles, which is hard enough, there are also powerful lobbyists who work on behalf of the oil companies, trying to weaken legislation and block the making of new laws altogether. They do this by telling lies and sowing confusion.

1. Look at this pie chart which shows the volume of heat-trapping gases that a selected number of countries release into the atmosphere (Source: Union of Concerned Scientists, 2020)

    a. Who should we be calling on to reduce their emissions of greenhouse gases?

    b. Should those countries that are not part of the problem (that is, whose CO2 emissions are already < 1 tonne per person per year) be allowed to carry on 'as normal'? Explain your answer.

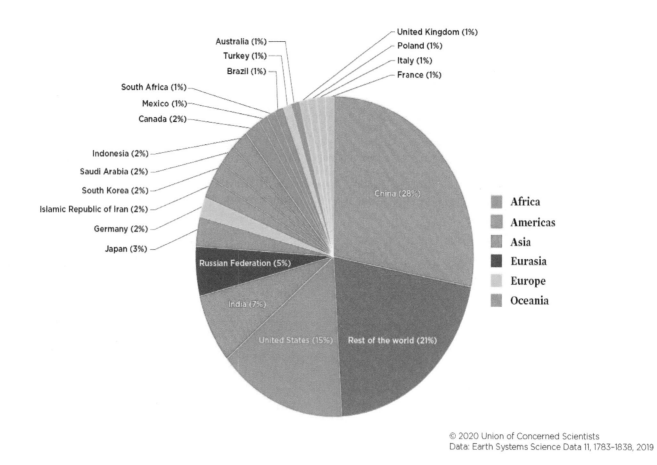

© 2020 Union of Concerned Scientists
Data: Earth Systems Science Data 11, 1783–1838, 2019

2. What degree of change to your own lifestyle are you prepared to put up with in order to minimise your carbon footprint? Are some areas of your life (e.g., fast food and foreign holidays) not up for negotiation?

Background

It can be found on beaches all over the world, it pollutes our oceans and harms our wildlife. Every minute of every day a truckload full of it gets dumped in the ocean, where wildlife eats it and gets tangled up in it. What is it? Plastic.

Plastic is anything that can be shaped when warm and soft, but which retains its shape when it hardens. It is made from a variety of raw materials but nowadays mainly **crude oil**. It has been around for a little over 100 years. In 1907, a Belgian chemist produced the first synthetic plastic from fossil fuels, but it was not until over fifty years later that it became ubiquitous - this word describes something that turns up everywhere. In the 1960s and 1970s your grandparents probably went to Tupperware parties where they marveled at the cheap,

unbreakable plastic boxes they could use around the kitchen. Then, in 1974, the first plastic drink bottles were made from PET (polyethylene terephthalate). No more taking empty lemonade bottles back to the shop to get your deposit back and spending it on sweets. Eventually this cheap, waterproof, unbreakable, washable material was everywhere, and we could not get enough of it.

Where are plastics used?

Plastic is used in hundreds of different ways. Most obviously, it is used to package dry foods, dairy, and meat products. It gets used to make single use plastic bags, disposable coffee cups and cutlery. Metal cans tend to be lined with it and it is also used to make glue and chewing gum. What is not so obvious, however, is that it is found in personal care products and kitchen sponges, in baby wipes and disposable nappies as well as in sanitary products, wrapping paper and many of the clothes that we wear.

So why did we fall out of love with plastic?

There are many reasons why plastic has fallen out of favour. The main problem is that it takes so long to decay. This means that when we've finished with it, it can't be easily disposed of. We like to think that it gets recycled, but, we can't be sure where it goes. Over twenty Olympic-sized swimming pools of plastic waste are exported from the UK every week and there is little way of knowing what happens to it. Sadly, there is reliable evidence that it gets buried in foreign landfill sites and leaks toxic waste. Or it gets burnt, polluting the air.

Then there is the problem of where it goes once it is discarded and the harm that it does there. Much of it finds its way to the sea, having been blown there or finding its way via rivers and sewers. It gets washed off our clothes and thrown away by fishermen. As many as 700,000 tiny fragments of microplastic can be found in a single load of washing and trawlers dump tonnes of abandoned fishing tackle including broken nets and ropes into the sea. Here, marine life gets tangled up in it and mistakes it for food. Sea birds, for example, when they find that they cannot digest the plastic bags, rings, cigarette lighters and wet wipes that they have eaten, starve to death because there is no room for the food that they ought to be eating that will nourish them. Even more worrying is that **microplastics** are getting into our food, where the chemicals that they contain mess up our internal organs, damage our immune systems and hinder reproduction and growth.

Could we cope without it?

While it might be difficult to eliminate plastic from our lives entirely, there are plenty of situations in which we use it where we could do without it altogether or swap it for something more environmentally friendly. Take packaging, for example. Supermarkets have already withdrawn all single use plastic bags from use, but many are now offering longer-lasting alternatives, including bags made from string, paper or jute. Wood can be used in the place of plastic in many cases, although there is not an infinite supply of this, either. You can buy wooden salad servers, and bamboo toothbrushes, too. Stainless steel and glass are also almost infinitely recyclable. Glass jars that contained coffee or jam when they were first bought can also be washed out and reused and while reusable cup made from bamboo or stainless steel could save thousands of plastic cups from landfill over a period of years. If you can move away from using cleaning products or toiletries and cosmetics that contain or are contained within plastic, you will be taking a step in the right direction. This might include buying cotton dish cloths rather than plastic sponges and rolls of paper towels or buying non-liquid soaps. Give washable nappies a go if you become a parent and you will be making huge strides. And having a different attitude to clothes can help, too. Being prepared to wear the same outfit on more than one occasion will reduce the demand for **synthetic fibres** such as polyester; and is it really such a chore to take your old clothes to a charity shop or to mend things rather than throw them away? You could even swallow your pride and start shopping there.

1. Do a plastics inventory around your school / classroom / bedroom / home

   a. What are you currently using plastic for when you could easily use some other material?

   b. Launch a campaign to reduce the use of plastic in your school.

2. 583.3 billion PET bottles were produced globally in 2021. That's almost 75 bottles for every person in the world.

   a. Why are so many of these PET bottles produced?

   b. What alternatives are there to using so many of them?

3. How could we clothe ourselves in a more environmentally friendly way?

4. Look out for an upcycling group you could join. Try your hand at turning something that someone was going to throw away into something worth keeping, or possibly even selling!

Background

Malaria is an infectious disease spread by mosquitoes that currently infects over 200 million people a year across much of South-East Asia and Sub-Saharan Africa. Of those 200 million, about half a million die, most of whom are children under the age of five. This is because their ability to fight off infection is weakened by not having had enough of the right things to eat, which we call **malnourishment**, or because their mothers caught the disease while pregnant. This meant that they were born before they were supposed to be and were not strong enough to fight off the many kinds of diseases that we would recover from. Scientists are having some success in fighting malaria, but there are often setbacks. For example, the number of people infected every year has fallen from 239 million in 2010 to 219 million in 2017 and the number of deaths from 607,000 to 435,000 over the same period. Since 2000, the number of countries affected has fallen from 106 to 86, cases have fallen by 36% and death rates by as much as 60%.

Why should we bother?

Experts disagree on whether **eradicating**, which means completely getting rid of, malaria is achievable, but those who think that it is possible estimate the cost to be about $100 billion (about £72 billion) over the next thirty years. For comparison, this is less than it costs to run the education system in the UK for a single year (£96 billion in 2020/21). Malaria is also judged to be the only one of the top ten killer diseases in the world that we have any chance of getting rid of.

The incentive to wipe out malaria is huge. Quite apart from the 500,000 lives that it would save every year, eliminating the disease would help to reduce **infant mortality**. It would also have a positive effect on education and the economy as fewer people would need to take time off work or school to recover from the illness. It is estimated, for example, that many billions of dollars are lost each year due to people being too sick to work. The amount that could be saved by 2040 as a result of people being able to work and not needing hospital treatment is estimated to be $2 trillion or £1.44 trillion. A trillion, by the way, is a million times a million. That's a lot of money!

So how can it be done?

There are three main ways in which malaria can be tackled: one is by stopping mosquitoes from breeding in the first place, the second is by stopping them from biting people and the third is with anti-malarial drugs and vaccines. We can prevent mosquitoes from breeding in several ways, for example by draining the stagnant bodies of water where this happens or by treating these sites with larvicides; these are chemicals that kill off the young wormlike forms of the insect so that they never mature into adults. There have also been some successful attempts at genetic mutation. This involves altering the code that the insects use to reproduce so that their offspring are **infertile**. Efforts to stop mosquitoes from biting people have included putting up screens in open doors and windows and encouraging people to sleep under mosquito nets treated with insecticide. The use of nets alone has increased from just 3% of the population of at-risk countries in 2004 to 44% in 2013. Many successful antimalarial drugs have been developed, and trials of an effective vaccine have also taken place.

What are the obstacles?

Unfortunately, the drugs that are taken by humans and insecticide sprays used to protect them only work for so long. As soon as the parasites become resistant to a particular drug or the insecticides fail to kill off at least 98% of the mosquitoes, they are deemed ineffective and the search to find a better solution must begin all over again. There are also a lot of bogus drugs on the market which mean that people are less likely to consent to treatment because they cannot be sure what exactly it is that they are taking and whether it might do them more harm than good. As for vaccines, these have struggled to reach even 50% effectiveness in reducing serious illness. This has made spending money on research into a vaccine for malaria look like a bit of a waste of time to wealthy investors. There is little chance of it making them very much money, after all. And, with malaria largely wiped out in the world's richest countries, who will spend their hard-earned cash on a project that they don't get to benefit from, at least not directly?

Poor access to effective health care is another obstacle to the eradication of malaria. Many who show symptoms of the disease cannot easily get to places where they can be diagnosed and treated. Nor can the nets which would protect people from being bitten be distributed to all the places where they are needed. Added to this, rising global temperatures mean that mosquitoes are becoming more widespread.

1.

    a. Based on the fall in the number of deaths and infections between 2010 and 2017, when might (i) infections and (ii) be reduced to zero.

    b. What are the limitations of using what we know about the past to predict the future?

2.

    a. You should be able to identify up to nine obstacles to the eradication of malaria from the text. Sort them - using the 'diamond model' if you like - from the most to the least challenging.

    b. Suggest how you might go about overcoming one or more of the obstacles.

Background

In 1994, following an earthquake, there was a massive power cut in Los Angeles. It plunged the entire city into darkness. That evening, the emergency services reported they had received hundreds of calls from concerned members of the public about a "strange white cloud in the sky". It was the Milky Way, our own galaxy, and the callers had never seen it before. Today, 83% of the world's population lives under light-polluted skies and this has risen by 2% every year between 2012 and 2016. There are lights everywhere. We work under them long after it has gone dark, play sports under floodlights during winter evenings and walk beneath the yellow glow of streetlamps at night. Soon, few of us will be able to see any stars at all.

What is light pollution?

We define **light pollution** as any artificial light that shines where it is neither wanted nor needed. **Sky glow** is the most significant kind. This is when the pink-orange light from cities spreads many miles beyond them because of sand, dust, and water droplets in the atmosphere. The bright lights of Las Vegas, for example, are scattered across eight national parks in the USA and smog, which is created when air is badly polluted, makes the situation even worse. Then there is wasted light to consider. This is light that either leaks directly into the sky without illuminating anything or which serves no real purpose other than, perhaps, for decoration. In the USA a staggering 13% of all the domestic electricity consumed is spent lighting the outside of our homes, while we live on the *inside*. In total, they waste $3 billion each year shining lights for nobody to see.

What are the effects of light pollution?

Light pollution affects both animals and the human population. Regarding animals, bright lights can play havoc with their reproduction, feeding and migration habits. For example, tens of thousands of migrating birds fly into the windows of skyscrapers in cities all over the world, disorientated by their brightly lit offices as people work on into the night. The bright lights from bars and hotels along the shoreline confuse turtle hatchlings who emerge from eggs buried beneath the beach. This often means that, instead of heading out to sea and relative safety, they head inland and are captured by their predators.

Light pollution is also bad news for people. It interferes with the production of melatonin, a chemical that the body produces when it is time to go to sleep; and leptin, another chemical that tells our digestive systems to slow down at night so that we don't wake up in the small hours craving for a roast dinner. If either of these is lacking, we will spend a lot of our time exhausted and hungry. Light saturation, which is when people are exposed to too much light, has also been shown to lead to a rise in certain cancers, most notably breast cancer.

So, what can we do?

Clearly, we cannot do without lights completely, but there are plenty of ways in which we can limit our use of lights and use them more efficiently. First, we must make as much use of natural daylight as we can. Take our work outdoors, move our desks over to the window if you must work in a building, and time your working day so that most of it is during daylight hours. Second, we must choose our lights more carefully. Incandescent bulbs, which gave off a lot of unwanted heat and not a

great deal of light are slowly being replaced by other kinds of lighting, including LEDs and solar-powered options. We can also use dimmers, voice activated switches and motion sensors to turn lights on and off as we enter and leave a room so that it is only lit when it is occupied. Even something as basic as switching the lights off in a room where nothing is happening helps enormously. Installing lighting at the lowest height that is effective works too because it means that all the light is focused on whatever it is you want to illuminate and less of it is reflected back into the sky or wasted lighting up things nobody wants to see.

On a larger scale, office lights could be timed to go off at the end of the working day. Streetlights could put on a time switch so that they turn off shortly after the pubs and clubs shut down and there is nothing on the streets but a few cats. This does raise questions about security so shop windows should only go dark when there is nobody walking by in the middle of the night to see them. Sporting events that usually take place under floodlights need to happen during daylight hours and we need to do away with decorative lights, other than temporarily for celebrations.

Being able to see the sky clearly at night and to be able to find complete darkness when we need it is important both for people and for animals. Not only does it enable us to wonder at how vast and complicated the universe is, but it also helps with navigation, especially on the open ocean where there are no other landmarks for reference.

1. Look at this graphic which shows the difference between various types of street lighting.

   a. On what basis are these judgements made?

   b. Could you think of a way of lighting the city streets at night that is both environmentally friendly, safe and cost effective?

2. Do some research into how you could minimise the wastage of light in your own home. How could you harness technology to help you?

3. Find out about the Bortle Scale of the Dark Sky. How would you rate the area where you live? Where have you been where you could see the night sky clearly?

Background

Leisure is not only taking up more of our time as we adjust to working less. It is also taking up more of our space and doing it at a time when there is less and less space available. When a generous guest editor who helped to finance the first copies of *Future Geographies* asked me to investigate the potential of closing down golf courses to solve the housing crisis, I was intrigued. So, this is what I found out.

Golf ... a waste of space?

After motorsport, golf uses up more space than any other leisure pursuit. In 2018, there were a total of 38,864 registered 18-hole courses in the world, an increase of around 4,500 on the 33,161 there were in 2016. This does not include pitch and putt courses, putting greens and driving ranges either, so the total number of golf-related facilities is probably much greater. This means that there are over 500,000 holes. If you played a different golf course every day it would take you about 75 years, which is close to an entire lifetime. Each

of these courses covers between 75 and 150 acres, which is about 30-

60 **hectares** (a **hectare** is about the same size as a football pitch at 10,000m^2). But golf appears to be declining in popularity, with 10 million people having given up the sport in the USA alone from 2002-2016. However, it has grown in terms of how much space it takes up. Although it is hard to make an accurate calculation, roughly 40,000 courses each taking up an average of 450,000 m^2 (0.45 km^2) means that 18,000 km^2 of the earth's surface is occupied by golf courses. This is about fifty times the size of the Isle of Wight or approximately the same area as all the islands that make up Fiji.

Is golf bad for the environment?

Quite apart from criticisms that golf is an elitist and sexist sport that is boring to watch and frustrating to play, there is plenty of evidence that golf is bad for the environment. For example, the vast amounts of water that are needed to maintain thousands of acres of manicured lawns in over 200 countries across the world contribute to water stress. 28 of the top 100 users of water in Las Vegas, for example, are golf courses. The golf industry is responsible for the use of tonnes of **fertiliser**s and **pesticides** each year which poison the water supply and reduce **biodiversity**. The impact of the 'golfication' of the landscape is most keenly felt in places where the local climate is very different to that which must be replicated in order for the game to be played. Building and maintaining them in the deserts of the Middle East and California, for example, is particularly challenging, quite apart from being a terrible waste of resources; all of which has led some critics of the sport to say it is a prime example of a wasteful and un**sustainable** approach to suburban development.

Golf courses ... the key to the housing crisis?

So, with the declining numbers of people playing golf and the supply of golf courses far outstripping demand, should the land be given up solving one of the greatest social problems of the 21st century, namely homelessness? The United Nations calculated in 2015 that roughly 100 million people were homeless. On a single night in 2017, a survey undertaken by the US government calculated that there were 553,700 such people in the United States. The UK homeless population stood at around 60,000 in 2017, with roughly 4,000 sleeping on the streets on any given night. For France, the overall figure was 150,000 in 2012, a 50% increase on 2001.

Certainly, homelessness is devastating, dangerous and isolating. According to Crisis, a homeless person is 17 times more likely to be a victim of violence and nine times as likely to commit suicide as a person with a secure home. One in three has been assaulted and almost one in every ten has been urinated on. More have been victims of theft than have escaped it.

Giving permission for housing to be built on golf courses would certainly appeal to some. As the majority are situated in the **rural-urban fringe**, any homes that were built would be within easy striking distance of a city with all its facilities and opportunities for employment. There would be some need to develop further **infrastructure**, for example by extending transport provision to deal with the increase in traffic. However, the increased population would also stimulate the local economy and, by means of the **multiplier effect**, create jobs, and increase prosperity. However, wealthy opponents would be bound to complain about the loss of **amenity**, the increased congestion, and the impact on property values, and would vigorously oppose any planning application through the courts.

One observer has noted that, in Los Angeles, the plight of the 60,000 homeless could be solved if all its golf courses were given over to housing. **Housing density**, that is how many houses are packed into any given space, is typically around 20 dwelling units per **hectare** (du/ha), which means that the typical course, at around 45 **hectare**s, could support 900 homes. With the average household being around two people, this means that each course could accommodate just short of 2,000 people. What is more, this would be the case if they were provided with substantial properties. Given much smaller apartments, much higher numbers could be catered for, although it might not be wise to attempt the 3,000 du/ha which is typical of the skyscrapers and tower blocks of Hong   Kong.

1. This table lists the world's top ten golfing nations and the number of recognised courses in each one.

   USA – 16,752

   Japan – 3,169

   Canada – 2,633

   England – 2,270

   Australia – 1,616

   Germany – 1,050

   France – 804

   South Korea – 798

   Sweden – 662

   Scotland – 614

   a. Using a blank map of the world, show this information in an appropriate format.

   b. What accounts for the popularity of golf in these countries in particular?

2. 'Golf causes huge environmental damage and brings little social or economic benefit for the majority'. To what extent do you agree with this statement?

3. 'Large open spaces should be set aside for the common good and not for the enjoyment of a small elite'. Discuss.

Background

If you have had the chance to look back at old family photographs, you might have noticed that previous generations had much larger numbers of children. Nowadays, in richer countries at least, families are much smaller. The average number of people per household has even fallen below 2.0. We call the number of live children that are born to the average woman who survives her childbearing years, which means they live until their mid-forties, the fertility rate. In 2020, this could have been as high as 7.1 (Nigeria) or as low as 1.0 (Korea). And, while driving down the birth rate in some countries where it is still very high is a good thing, half the countries in the world now have fertility rates below the 'magic' figure of 2.1. We call this the **replacement rate** as, when the fertility rate falls below this figure, populations begin to shrink.

Surely that's good? Aren't there too many people, anyway?

There is certainly a sense in which a reduced fertility rate is good news. When fewer babies are born in a country, it costs less to bring them up and educate them, so we can spend money on other priorities such as investing in health and transport. It is also good for the environment as every person born is a consumer of energy and resources. Yet there comes a tipping point when too few people are being born. Eventually, the relatively low number of workers becomes a problem. Their elders outnumber them and there are more old people needing care than there are young people who can provide it. If you've heard of the Demographic Transition Model, this is what we refer to as Stage 5.

How did it get like this?

People are put off having children for all kinds of reasons. One of the first reasons why families shrank in the early twentieth century in the UK was that there was no need to have 'extra' children to help with manual work such as farming. Nor, once they introduced the state pension in 1909 were they needed to support people who were too old to work. Later on, as women accounted for a greater share of the workforce, they had them to juggle their homes and careers, so they had less time for family life. More recently, people have given other reasons, often revolving around parents' concerns for the future quality of life of children born into a world that they perceive to be in crisis, or around the expense of having children. Others say that they don't feel there is enough support for young adults who are trying to bring up families of their own.

For some women, the choice is a far more personal one. Some do not want to go through the physical pain of childbirth or see children as being an obstacle to having a successful career. Others want children but don't want husbands. A minority has a problem with relationships per se and doesn't want to get involved in them for fear of getting caught up in domestic violence or revenge pornography. This is when, usually after a relationship has ended, the rejected partner shares explicit details and photographs of their relationship with a third party to embarrass or shame the person who dumped them. Women in Korea even have a word - *sampo* - to describe those who have decided to live a life without sexual relations, marriage, or children. Finally, there are those who choose not to have children as a way of leading a more **sustainable** life. One less child, after all, means fewer clothes to wash, smaller cars to drive, and about 5,000 fewer nappies sent to landfill sites.

Can't we change their minds?

If we want to stop the fertility rate from declining further, there are two things that need to be done. First, we must make sure that nobody opts out of having children because they cannot afford it. Then, we need to reconcile the demands of work with those of family life so that it is possible for people to do both things at once.

Hungary has put forward one of the most radical ideas. Referring to itself as "family-friendly" in an ongoing advertising campaign that uses up quite a chunk of the national budget, it offers several incentives for young couples to have three or more children. Women under the age of 40, for example, can apply for what are referred to as "baby expecting loans" of up to £25,000 for each child. Those who have three children within a certain time frame do not even have to make any repayments and the birth of the fourth child makes a woman exempt from income tax for life. In South Korea, all parents with children under the age of eight may clock off from work one hour earlier each day while, in Singapore, young couples can access what they call a "proximity housing grant". This provides financial assistance to young couples who want to live within 4 km of their parents so that their parents can help provide childcare as opposed to them having to rely on the state.

How this will all play out over the decades ahead is hard to predict. As one commentator has put it, governments cannot dictate what happens in the bedroom. Rather, what happens in the bedroom determines what governments should do.

1. This chart (Source: Our World in Data) shows the change in fertility rates for several countries in the world

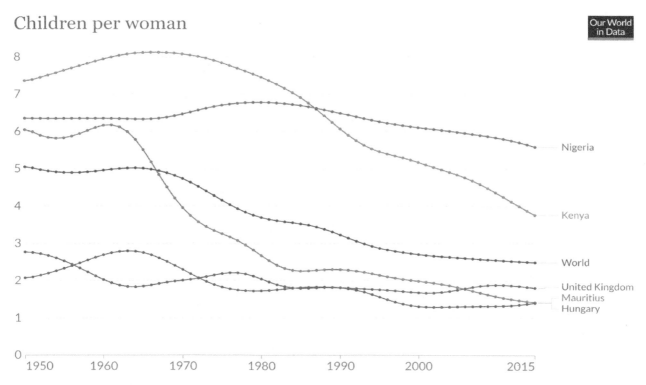

Children per woman

Source: United Nations – Population Division (2019 Revision)   OurWorldInData.org/fertility-rate • CC BY
Note: Children per woman is measured as the total fertility rate, which is the number of children that would be born to the average woman if she were to live to the end of her child-bearing years and give birth to children at the current age-specific fertility rates.

 a. Which country had the highest fertility rate in 2015?

 b. Which countries are currently below 'replacement level'?

 c. Can you think why fertility rates rose in the UK from around 1950-1965?

2.

 a. What are your own thoughts about having children in the future?

 b. If people are inclined not to have them should others try to persuade them to change their minds by financial or other means? Explain your answer.

3. "People who choose not to have children are selfish." Discuss.

Background

As if the rapid increase in the world's population, which has almost reached eight billion, were not enough to worry about, there is also another equally pressing problem. This is the increase in the global **dependency ratio**. This is a statistic that tells us how well balanced a population is. Are there, for example, large numbers of children and not enough adults to provide for them? Or, perhaps, there is an imbalance between the number of people of working age and the number of people who have retired? It could even be a combination of both.

The **dependency ratio** (DR) is calculated as follows:

$$\frac{number\ of\ children\ under\ 15\ (c)\ +\ number\ of\ adults\ over\ 64\ (e)}{the\ number\ of\ adults\ of\ working\ age\ (w)}$$

Values across the world vary considerably. China, for example, has a DR of 42.0, largely on account of One-Child Policy it implemented in the 1980s, while Niger has a DR of 109.5 The figure for the UK is around 57.0 and the average for the whole world is around 53.7. This means that, for every 100 in the world people of working age, there are just over 53 people who rely on them to pay for their pensions, their health and personal care and their education.

Why is the dependency ratio rising and why does it matter?

The **dependency ratio** is affected by the birth rate and by life expectancy. A high birth rate, all other things being equal, will lead to a high DR. This, in turn, tends to slow down economic growth because providing health care for and educating so many children takes a large chunk out of the country's tax revenues. A high life expectancy will cause other kinds of problems as large numbers of people who become too old to work stop paying their taxes and, instead need their pensions paying and their health costs met. This often means that the state ends up borrowing large amounts of money and getting into serious debt.

By contrast, a country with a low DR can look forward to economic growth. With relatively few people to educate and fewer hospital bills and pensions to pay, the state can invest the money that it takes in tax in other ways of improving people's quality of life.

So, can we influence the dependency ratio?

There is only so much that can be done to influence a country's **dependency ratio** in the short to medium term. Though, in theory, it would be possible, it clearly isn't ethical to deliberately reduce the number of elderly people! Birth rates, on the other hand, can be reduced, chiefly by educating and empowering women so that the fertility rate, that is the number of children born to each woman, falls.

What can be done is to make sure that people start to plan for their later years and that they start doing so sooner. Those who want to enjoy a lengthy retirement will inevitably have to pay more into their pension pots, investing a large chunk of what they earn throughout their working lives. Already, in Australia for example, employees are required to put 9% of their earnings to one side for later life. Neither can we assume an automatic right to stop working at a particular age. Employees will have to become much more flexible in this regard and people's perceptions of what counts as work

and deserves to be paid will have to change. Your parents might have expected your grandparents to provide childcare for you because your grandparents had retired soon after you were born. But will you be able to call on your parents to look after your children? After all, they may still be working themselves. The state will also have to think ahead, building more hospitals and care homes and training up people to work in adult care and to specialise in **gerontology**, which is the scientific study of old age, the process of ageing, and the particular problems of old people.

An altogether different attitude towards the elderly is called for. Research suggests that they are not, generally, well respected, particularly in high-income countries (HICs). As many as one elderly person in six has even reported being abused. What is more, their poor treatment affects their mental and physical health. They are then portrayed as frail, dependent and out of touch, which only serves to make people think even less of them. We need to change society's attitude towards the elderly such that their contributions continue to be valued long after they have retired from full-time work. Then they can begin to retain their dignity. This will harness their skills and wisdom and unlock their potential. We also need to be creative about how we support our elderly dependent population, creating networks and support groups that will allow them to live with a certain degree of independence rather than isolating them from much of the rest of society in hospitals and care homes.

1. Here is the population structure of Mauritius, a small island in the Indian Ocean with a population of around 1.3 million.

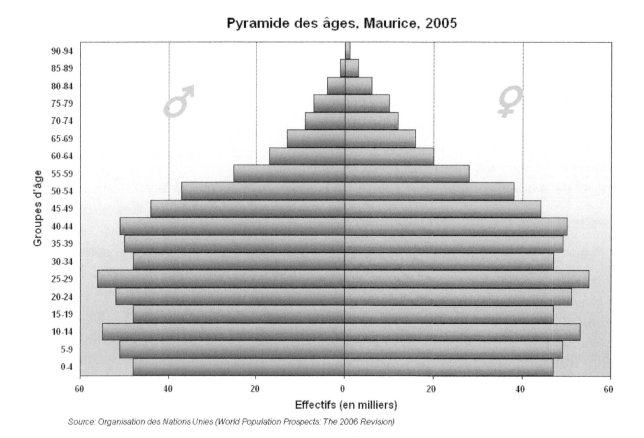

Source: Organisation des Nations Unies (World Population Prospects: The 2006 Revision)

a. Which are the largest age groups on the island?

b. Do you suppose Mauritius has a high dependency ratio or a low one? Justify your answer from the population pyramid.

c. Imagine it is now 30 years from now. Life expectancy is already 74 years in 2021 and the fertility rate is 1.4 births per woman.

    i.   Sketch a population pyramid for the year 2060.

    ii.   What challenges do you anticipate Mauritius will face at that time?

    iii.   What can the country do to be ready for them?

Background

Living in a city was once the exception rather than the rule. A small number have existed since ancient times as centres of administration, learning, trade, and worship. Yet it was only with the arrival of the Industrial Revolution, which started in Britain in around 1760, that they became the places where most people lived because they had to go and work in nearby factories. Since then, **urbanisation** has continued apace. In the UK, 83.9% of the population live in urban areas (2019), while, in the world, the figure now stands at 56.2% (2020).

So, why all the fuss?

Properly managed towns and cities are, potentially, very efficient places to live because they provide for so many people in relatively little space. However, without proper planning and control, many in LICs are fast becoming overcrowded while others in HICs are being deserted. There is therefore the possibility that many megacities in the Global South will soon be overwhelmed with slums and environmental problems. There, **counterurbanisation**, which is the movement of people from the city back into the countryside, is almost unheard of. This is because there are too many people working in the informal sector, doing jobs that cannot be done remotely. They do not have the option of leaving the city. In contrast, parts of cities in the Global North will become deserted as those who no longer need to live in them, because they are working remotely, or can afford to commute long distances, choose to live elsewhere.

All cities, whether in HICs or LICs, use up more than their share of resources, including 75% of available global energy. They feed people's desire for more products and services, which we call **consumerism**, and create millions of tonnes of waste every day. In Mumbai, for example, 11,000 tonnes of waste are dumped in the city daily which only serves to pollute the environment and spread disease. And, in both rich cities and poor cities, some **infrastructure** is fast becoming obsolete, either because it is reaching the end of its useful life or because it is having to cope with more commuters, water and waste than it was ever designed to handle.

What can be done?

The answer, in both cases, lies in making urban environments more **sustainable**, that is they can meet the needs of the people who live there today without messing things up for those who will live there in the future. The cities of the past were judged based on how much money they generated and how weird their skyscrapers were. In contrast, those of the future will be judged according to the quality of their parks and green spaces. It will also be important for them to be resilient and efficient, to respond to change quickly, to have a smaller **carbon footprint** and to find ways of repurposing redundant buildings and **infrastructure**. Already in London, for example, old railway cuttings and sidings have been transformed into green spaces, while the ten miles of underground tunnels that were abandoned by Royal Mail trains have been repurposed as a visitor experience and used to grow mushrooms. The Chinese have even made visiting landfill sites part of the tourist experience!

The future of the city centre

While the problem in LICs remains that too many people want to live there, the reverse is true of many towns and cities in the Global North. Here, traffic congestion, run-down high streets, pollution, and the convenience of shopping online have all combined to deliver nothing but store closures, job losses and empty pavements. In Great Britain alone, the COVID pandemic contributed to the disappearance of more than 11,000 outlets from its high streets, shopping centres and retail parks in 2020.

Whether or not 'rich' cities can recover from this downturn depends on whether their centres can be repurposed to serve all the needs of their surrounding communities rather than just being turned back into the shopping deserts that they were in the late 20th century. Large buildings that are no longer needed by the huge anchor stores that used to draw people into town centres, need to be converted into residential units. Urban authorities also need to promote the mixed use of city centres, blending shops with medical centres, restaurants, cafes, and entertainment venues to give people a variety of reasons to visit them.

Another deciding factor will be how well they can respond to the challenge of managing their waste. Here options include incinerating it to generate energy. A tonne of waste, for example, can generate 0.3 megawatts of electricity, which would be enough to supply around 300 homes with the power they need for one hour, depending on the level of demand. Plans to turn waste into building blocks are also underway, much as was predicted in the movie *WALL-E*, making it possible that, in the near future, new structures will be made entirely from recycled materials.

Finally, there is the issue of whether town and city centres can resist the temptation to become '**clone towns**' and instead establish or re-establish their own sense of identity. The term '**clone town**' came to be used of urban areas that had no unique characteristics and whose high streets and retail parks were taken over by chain stores. The resurfacing of independent stores along with cultural and sporting events such as the Commonwealth Culture initiative (Coventry, 2021) may be able to act as catalysts for change in this respect. Indeed, as I write this, my hometown of Coventry is rediscovering its past and reimagining its future as it lives out its year in the spotlight as the UK's City of Culture 2021.

Games (Birmingham 2022) and the Cities of

1. Look at this chart which shows the trend in store closures on the UK high street since 2015

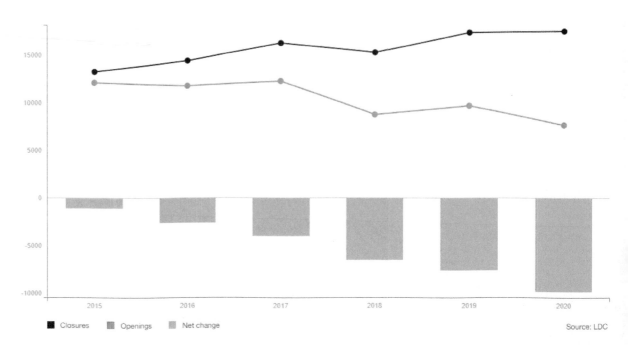

   a. Describe the patterns that it shows.

   b. Do you think that this spells the end for the high street as we know it? Why? Why not?

2. Much as they might like to escape from the city, few people living in the Global South have this option.

   a. Explain why this is the case.

   b. What can be done to make life in the city more tolerable for those who do not have the option of returning to the countryside?

3. Assuming you live in a town or city, can you identify any buildings or abandoned spaces that could be repurposed? What would you do to make your town more sustainable?

Background

Out of a total global population of around 7.9 billion people (2021), just over a quarter of a billion, or 272 million, are not living in the country where they were born. And while many of them move out of choice, for work, for family reasons or to study, increasing numbers are being forced into leaving by violence, **climate change** and natural disasters. Indeed, the number of **refugees** and internally displaced people (those who are made to leave their homes yet remain in the same country) has doubled between 2010 and 2020 according to the World Migration Report. In terms of the number of migrants that it accepts, the UK ranks 5th in the world, with only the USA, Germany, Saudi Arabia and Russia taking on more.

Beware the closing doors

However, allowing people to go wherever they want to can cause problems and this has led to many countries deciding to be much stricter about who they let in or keep out. Many people in the UK, for example, now feel very strongly about this and it was probably one of the most important reasons why they voted to leave the European Union in June 2016. Furthermore, there is a Bill going through the UK Parliament in July 2021 that will make it a criminal offence punishable by up to four years in prison to arrive in the UK without permission. This increases to life imprisonment for those found guilty of people smuggling.

On the one hand, there are those who want to control our borders more tightly and allow fewer people to settle here. They argue that allowing too many migrants to enter the country puts too much pressure on public services such as schools, hospitals, and housing. They object to newcomers who they think are taking their jobs and claiming benefits from a system to which they have contributed nothing. Some are even worried that allowing people into the UK from certain countries might make the UK a less safe place as new arrivals may have links with countries and organisations with which we are not on good terms.

Others are more welcoming of migrants, particularly the small but increasing numbers of people who are fleeing violence, political unrest, and natural disasters. They say that we need the skills and abilities of people from all over the world to continue to prosper. In 2020, for example, 170,000 of the 1.28 million people employed by our NHS were not British. Opponents to tighter border controls also say that it is wrong not to offer opportunities and the chance of a better quality of life to those who would otherwise be caught up in conflict and corruption.

Some countries try to control migration by using a points system where potential migrants are assessed against a set of criteria to determine who may enter. This is the case in Australia, where someone who wanted to settle in the country would stand a much better chance of being accepted if they had certain skills that were in short supply, spoke English and were below a certain age. This last rule is designed to make sure that migrants have enough of their working lives remaining when they arrive. In this way, the government can be fairly certain that they will pay a fair amount of money in taxes before they start becoming a financial burden, either by becoming ill and needing healthcare and/or retiring and being entitled to a pension.

More desperation, more deaths

It should come as no surprise, therefore, that not everyone keeps to the rules about who may and may not enter a country. What is more, hundreds of people now risk their lives every day crossing busy shipping lanes such as the English Channel, which is less than 20 miles wide at its narrowest point, and the Strait of Gibraltar where the gap between Europe and Africa is a little over nine miles. In 2020 coastguards rescued over 16,000 people trying to reach Spain but by mid-2021 they had already intercepted 22,000. From 1995-2010, at least 5,000 died attempting the crossing and many of their bodies were washed ashore. If they were lucky, they may have received a hasty burial. In 2010, the asking price for a ticket to cross the Straits of Gibraltar was around $1,000. But there are plenty of people whose attempts to feed themselves and their families in Morocco have come to nothing, who are willing to pay up, even though this is like asking someone on average earnings in the UK to pay £5,000 for a one-way ticket on a ferry from Portsmouth to the Isle of Wight. The actual price was £14.00 in July 2021.

1. These statistics compare Morocco and Spain. The data is from 2010.

	Morocco	Spain
Net migration (people gained or lost per million per year)	-720	+990
Population (millions)	34.8	40.5
Life Expectancy at birth	74	84
GDP per capita	$4,100	$30,100
Unemployment (%)	10.2	8.3
Mobile phones in use	16.0 million	26.1 million
Internet Users	6.1 million	18.6 million

a. What evidence is there in this table that quality of life is better for most people in Spain than it is in Morocco?

b. Design an information board to be displayed either on the beaches of Northern France or Morocco that would make people think twice about crossing to the UK/Spain.

2. Some borders are much more tightly controlled than others. Suggest why this might be.

3. How might hostility towards migrants backfire on a country that controls its borders very tightly? Should we, therefore, be more welcoming towards migrants?

Background

One of the most famous stories in the Bible tells of a conflict between the Israelites and one of their most feared enemies, the Philistines. You may not remember the details, if indeed you ever knew them, but the story of David and Goliath and how the 'little guy' won against all the odds tells us what warfare was like in the past. Two clearly defined armies faced one another across a relatively short distance and used what, by our standards, would be seen as very limited technology to take the other side out. Open conflict was the norm. Fast forward about three thousand years and the situation has changed completely. David doesn't square up to Goliath across a traditional battlefield anymore; and the tactics that he uses are much more devious and unpredictable than they used to be. War in the 21st century will be a very different prospect.

War in the past

For as long as there have been different nations, tribes, and empires there have been wars. Our ancestors fought with sharpened sticks and rocks and fought one another in hand-to-hand conflict. Even as recently as one hundred years ago very little had changed except that the weapons involved had become more accurate and the distances between opposing armies were measured in miles rather than yards. Wars were 'declared' and fought between entire nations and groups of nations; each being represented by an army. They were contested out in the open, each side trying to annihilate the other's military capabilities. Everyone knew the score.

What changed?

The first sign that wars would be fought very differently from the middle of the 20th century onwards came on 6 August 1945 when the first atomic bomb was dropped on Hiroshima. Here was a new weapon that could be used to wipe out entire cities indiscriminately. This raised the prospect that simply having more guns and more soldiers than your opponent would not always guarantee victory. Technology had arrived on the battlefield. The mid-20th century also saw an increase in **terrorist** activity. This is the politically motivated use or threat of violence to attract publicity for a particular cause. This meant that the distinction between the 'weak' and the 'strong' became blurred.

The battlefield was once a clearly defined physical space (e.g., the Battle of Hastings or the Battle of the Somme), battles could now be fought anywhere from busy shopping centres to public transport networks. and it became much harder to know where your enemies were, and even who they were. Rather than targeting the enemy's military capabilities and leaving ordinary civilian people out of the equation, terrorism seeks to make people feel insecure through random acts of violence on ordinary people. **Terrorist**s do this in the hope that they will get a reaction from their enemies that will allow them to portray them as the real aggressors and so make the **terrorist**s' cause look legitimate.

In the future, some wars will also be fought remotely, whether with unmanned drones or long-range missiles. The distances between opposing groups will increase as each tries to outdo the other, bragging to the world's media about the range of their latest weapon. This way of waging war is cost-effective, too, as it doesn't involve moving tanks, ships, and aircraft halfway around the world. And, often, the mere threat of force is enough to keep an enemy at bay, particularly if that threat involves the use of nuclear weapons far more powerful than the ones that were dropped on Japan in 1945.

Cyber warfare is also on the increase. In the future, countries will fight some of their wars without having to put their own people in harm's way. They will not face their enemies in the way that their ancestors used to. Neither will they target their opponents' military forces for the most part. Rather they will seek to cripple their opponents by attacking their **infrastructure** remotely, paralysing their energy grids, transport networks and industrial facilities to bring down their economy. Indeed, this is already happening on such a large scale, with hackers distributing viruses and malware, that we must assume that at least some of the activity is state-sponsored.

Some wars will, however, still be played out in specific locations. These may be places where otherwise scarce resources are up for grabs, for example oil or rare minerals, or where poor or corrupt governance has provided a place for **extremists** to come together in large numbers. This, in part, explains why the Middle East is and will continue to be a volatile part of the world as, not only does it provide the world with huge amounts of oil, but also it is a place where people of many different religious and political persuasions live in close proximity. The world's few as yet unclaimed spaces are also likely candidates as future battlefields, especially the wilderness areas that may hold precious resources, such as Antarctica and the Arctic Ocean. This raises the prospect of countries increasingly having to fight their battles a long way from home to preserve their interests. Indeed, there is a fear in some circles that there will be an increasing number of conflict zones like these. This might mean that even the forces of a superpower, such as the United States, could be spread so thinly over the world as to make it vulnerable to attack on many different fronts. Some say that such fears were partly to blame for the US withdrawal from Afghanistan in 2021.

1. In what kinds of places is war likely to break out in the 21st century? What can governments do to prepare for these conflicts?

2. Check out the website https://www.cfr.org/global-conflict-tracker/?category=us.

   a. Describe the distribution of threats to the United States as shown on the map.

   b. How might even a superpower find it impossible to fight on all these fronts at the same time?

3. What are the implications for future conflicts of not knowing who your enemy is or where they are?

Background

There are a few areas in the world that are true wilderness. Until the middle of the twentieth century, most people were content to leave them alone. After all, places such as the Amazon Rainforest, the Sahara Desert and the Tibetan Plateau were extremely inhospitable. They were also too inaccessible, and few people thought that there was anything valuable there. Fast forward half a century and many of these places have suddenly become of interest, especially to countries who have their eyes on greater power or more resources. One such place is the Arctic. This is the area that lies north of the Arctic Circle and includes the much of the coastlines of Russia, Iceland, the USA, Canada, and Greenland. It also includes a vast ocean and several strategically placed islands.

Whose is interested in this icy wilderness?

Several countries have an interest in the Arctic. These include Canada, the country with the longest coastline in the world, Russia, Iceland, Denmark (which owns Greenland), and the USA. They also have several reasons to get involved. First, they want to exploit the region's potential as a source of valuable resources such as gold, fish, oil, uranium, and natural gas. Second, they want to establish a military presence in the area for reasons of national security. Third, they want access to any shipping routes that might open up as the ice melts. These include the North Sea Route, which runs along the north coast of Russia, and the Northwest Passage, which offers a way of getting from the North Atlantic to the North Pacific that is 5000km shorter than going via the Panama Canal. It is also a region that interests scientists, explorers, and tourists.

The legal status of the mainland that extends beyond the Arctic Circle and most of the islands that are dotted across the oceans is clear - they are owned by one of the interested countries. With the ocean, however, it gets rather complicated. Gaps between some Canadian islands, for example, are large enough for international waters to exist between them. This would mean that they could, in theory, be used to establish shipping lanes that would be open to all. This was certainly what the USA believed to be the case when they sneaked through the Northwest passage without asking Canada's permission.

Why now?

Until recently, the risks of venturing into the Arctic outweighed the rewards; there was too much to lose and little to be gained. Canada's government, for example, once neglected many of its more remote islands. But now that there is the prospect of large expanses of the ocean melting in the summer months, these areas have become strategically important. Tension has also been building over recent years. For example, the Russians have manned a research base close to the North Pole for several years and have blown the dust off many research bases along their northern coastline that were abandoned as the Cold War thawed. Observers also suspect that they have sent submarines deep below the ocean ice. As recently as 2014, they planted their flag in a titanium capsule on the seabed, which only made the other Arctic nations angry.

Will this lead to anything more serious?

It seems unlikely that this saber-rattling, that is a show of military might, will lead to anything that we ought to be worried about soon. It would mess up many valuable opportunities for co-operating in scientific research and there are plenty of organisations to help rival nations resolve their disputes without having to resort to blowing one another up. Neither does the presence of armed forces of a region mean that an aggressive nation is gearing up for invasion, even though much of the media would like us to believe it. Besides, Russia's armed forces are only a shadow of what they used to be back in the days of the USSR, and the extreme cold would make it difficult to sustain military operations there. As one US commander pointed out, you would be fighting two wars at once, one against your enemy and another against the cold.

However, we cannot rule out the possibility of rising tensions in the Arctic leading to something more serious. In 2018, both Russia, and NATO and its allies played out a series of war games in the region. The NATO exercises took place in Norway, very close to where the Russians keep many of their nuclear weapons. Participants were asked to play out their likely response to a Russian invasion of Norway with the help of many thousands of armed vehicles, while the Russians took 300,000 troops to the far east of the country to play out the possible consequences of NATO and its allies declaring war against them. The United States is reopening its bases in Iceland to assert its presence in the Northern Atlantic and is also building new icebreakers to replace its ageing fleet, supposedly so that it can keep open routes through the frozen oceans for as long as possible. Meanwhile, the Russians are rebuilding their navy in Murmansk, the only one of their ports that has direct year-round access to the North Atlantic Ocean and both the USA and Russia are increasing their stockpiles of nuclear weapons.

Things to do

1. Consider this map of the Arctic Ocean, which shows some of the trade routes that could open up as the ocean melts (Source: The Arctic Institute)

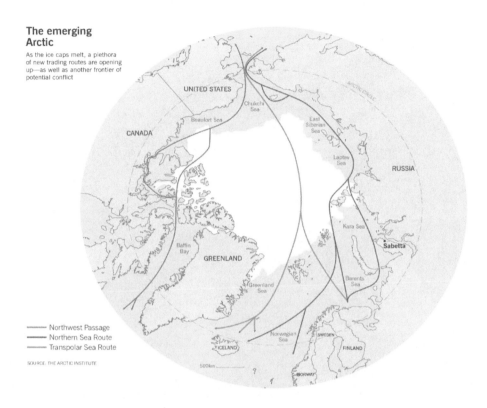

   a. How would these routes benefit international trade?

   b. What environmental damage might be caused when using them?

2. What are some challenges of policing an area as vast as the Arctic? Is there any way in which we can solve them?

3. Do you think we can share the resources that are found in the Arctic Ocean? If not, how will we decide what belongs to whom.

Background

Some people think that the world might be a better place if it had a single government. It is an idea that goes back many centuries, and it has enjoyed newfound popularity at certain times during the last century, partly because of the two world wars and the difficulties we have had managing the recent COVID pandemic. In 1945, the nuclear bombs that were dropped on Japan brought an end to World War II. This made people even more determined to bring in a new world order to make future conflict less likely. The famous physicist, Albert Einstein, even remarked back then that there would either be "one world or no world at all". Then, in the 1960s, the idea went rather quiet. This was when the Cold War made the West very suspicious of the USSR - an alliance of Soviet states that existed until 1992. But now that these relations have thawed a little, the question is being asked once again and even promoted by respected institutions and politicians, both past and present. In 2021, for example, the Olympic motto, "Faster, higher, stronger" has had the word "together" added at the Summer Games in Tokyo.

How could it come about?

A global government could only come about in one of two ways: either by mutual agreement or by one country or superpower, forcing its will on the rest of the world. Many think that this makes it unlikely that we will ever have a World President as, despite the many advantages that it would bring, there would also be many problems. As one commentator has said, we have reached a point in history where the nations of the world need each other but do not trust one another. There would be too much disagreement about how to organise a single government, no consensus about what its priorities should be or about the mechanics of making them happen. Besides, a government only works when it knows its people well.

Others point out that many international organisations already exist and that a single world government is a natural development of this. The lessons of history have not stopped us from trying to achieve it, either. The ancient Egyptians aspired to rule over "everything the sun touched" and Hitler had similar aspirations for Nazi Germany.

What are the advantages?

There are many advantages to setting up a single government for the entire world. First, it would reduce inequality as people and resources would be free to move around as they pleased. Everything would be cheaper and there would be a single currency for all. There would be no more **refugees**, at least in theory, and no more blaming other people or passing the buck when it came to solving environmental issues such as **global warming**. From an economic perspective, a single government would solve a lot of problems, too, as we would pay all our taxes, which would be levied at a uniform rate, to a single authority. Tax dodging and tax havens would become a thing of the past. A single world government would also mean that there would be a fair and measured response to crises while nuclear weapons, indeed weapons of any kind, would be redundant. On paper, at least, nobody would have any enemies. Without enemies, we could stop worrying about defence and security, too, and focus our efforts on health and education, which would accelerate development.

It's not as easy as that

The chief obstacle to a world ruled by one government is that, for it to happen, groups of people with different values, beliefs and cultures would have to set aside some if not all their differences. Were this to happen, many parts of the world would 'go beige', losing their distinct identity completely and becoming non-places where everyone drinks Coca Cola, wears Nike trainers, eats fast food and has everything delivered by Amazon. We call this cultural erosion. It would also be impossible for there to be a level playing field over the entire world. Differences in the physical landscape, resources and climate would mean some places were always more prosperous than others. Neither could we easily overcome the burden of history with all its past conflicts and injustices and get people who used to be enemies to cooperate. Then, there is the question of how we would administer a global government, who would determine and enforce its policies, and decide where its capital might be. To whom would the government be accountable and by what means? And even though it might appear to be a **democracy** from the outside, it would be very difficult for such a large organisation to take on everyone's views. Were this to be the case, the world would end up being run in the interests of an influential minority, anyway.

1. This graph shows a comparison of Comprehensive National Power (CNP) for six selected countries. This statistic combines information about a country's armed forces, its economic prosperity and the influence of its culture. It is an indicator of the probability that it will

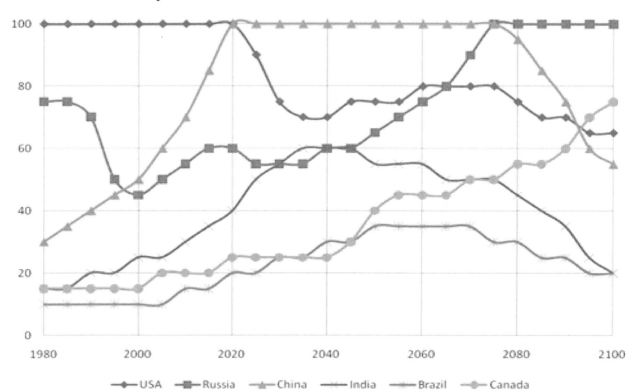

Comprehensive National Power 1980-2100

become a superpower.

    a. Which country is expected to dominate

        i.   From 1980 until 2020?

        ii.   From 2020 until 2070?

        iii. From 2070 onwards?

    b. How credible do you think these predictions are?

    c. Do you think any one single country will ever have the power to dominate the entire world?

    d. Is there any scenario in which every country might choose to cooperate with all the others?

2. This article, adapted from an American website, considers Vladimir Putin's chances of making Russia the great nation it once was.

Putin has never been shy in declaring his intentions to restore Russia back to its former superpower glory and is actively trying to recreate the former empire. […] While there are several very convincing facts that underscore Russia's influential position in the world (i.e. the world's largest energy producer of **crude oil**, a primary exporter of natural gas to Europe, a balanced budget if oil prices stay over $100 a barrel, a permanent seat on the United Nations Security Council, and boosting one of the world's strongest nuclear arsenals), it is only just that: an influential power—and not a superpower.

Putin ambitions to mark a return of Russia to its former "Great Power" glory require someone to whom Russia can sell its energy and an external threat to rally its people, […] If the West isolates an increasingly stubborn Putin, he will turn to China for "secondhand technology" as he needs to modernize. While the Russian military-industrial complex needs a serious makeover, make no mistake it is still intact and can be rebuilt but this can only be done at a severe cost on the living conditions of the Russian people. Putin will not survive a deterioration of Russian income per capita wealth and freedom at the same time. Thus, in the end, nothing will really change much. Russia will continue to be influential but not a superpower: Russia will stay Russia.

Does this article support the idea that Russia will soon be a superpower? Give your evidence.

Background

Have you ever noticed how much smaller our grandparents' wardrobes are than our own? This is because, over the last fifty years, the number of items of clothing in the average wardrobe has increased by 500%. Now, in a single year, it is not unusual for well over 100 billion items of clothing to be sold along with almost 15 billion pairs of shoes. Even more alarming is the rate at which it is thrown away - an entire dustbin lorry full of wasted clothes every single second.

Why has this happened?

All this has happened because of the rise of fast fashion; a global industry that produces poor quality, trendy clothing which tries to replicate what celebrities and fashion models are wearing only for consumers to wear the items a few times before throwing them away. This vast enterprise, driven by social media influencers and multinational companies, has altered people's perception of what is acceptable when it comes to what we wear and how quickly we ought to discard it. Today, one-third of 16-24-year-old females, for example, believe that a garment that has been worn more than a couple of times is 'old'. Nor does it help that, after being worn and washed a few times, these almost disposable clothes already look faded, worn and out of shape.

What is the impact of 'fast fashion'?

Fast fashion is bad news on many fronts, both economic, environmental, and social. It is bad news for the environment because it is resource hungry. For example, it takes 20,000 litres of water to process a single kilogram of cotton and the washing, solvents and dyes involved account for around 20% of all industrial water pollution. It also contributes more to **climate change** than aviation and shipping combined. It is responsible for 25% of all **pesticide** use, a quarter of all the **microplastics** in the oceans and 8% of all **carbon emissions**. Neither does it stop there. Less than 20% of all clothing manufacturers have a clear recycling policy, so 60% of fast fashion ends up in landfill sites. Here, as over half of it is made from polyester, it takes over 200 years to decompose.

Socially, fast fashion is also a disaster. This is because it creates more demand for poorly regulated factories, sometimes known as **sweatshop**s. Here workers, including children who really ought to be in school, are badly treated, have little or no job security and get paid very little. Accidents in workplaces with few, if any, health and safety measures in place have resulted in many people losing their lives. This is also true of the largely unregulated use of **fertiliser**s and **pesticides** on cotton which some claim has caused many more deaths.

Finally, there is the economic cost of all this waste to consider. It has been suggested, for example, that as much as $500 billion per year is lost because clothing is underutilised and there is no way of recycling it effectively.

What can be done?

There needs to be both a personal and corporate response to the problems caused by fast fashion. On a personal level, we can always opt for clothes that have been made under tighter regulations to try and phase out the use of **sweatshop**s and protect the environment. People can reduce their demand for clothing by buying second-hand clothing and/or donating the clothes that they no longer want or need to charity shops or via online platforms. Clothes sharing is another option in which groups of people agree to pool their wardrobes; the only trouble with this being that it won't work for people whose size or shape falls outside the normal range. Clothing rental, which was once only for weddings and other special occasions, is becoming more widespread. And you can always make or

repair your own clothes, or repurpose them, for example by cutting down an old pair of jeans whose knees are worn through to make some shorts … or by tearing down the curtains in your bedroom to make play clothes for your children as was the case in *The Sound of Music*!

Future Fabrics

At a corporate level, there is also much that can be done. Fashion chains need to provide the incentive to recycle clothes. Some already do this by working in partnership with charities. There also needs to be more investment in **sustainable** fabrics, whether this is through the reuse of traditional materials such as cotton and wool, or by developing new ones. Linen, for example, which grows from flax seeds, can be produced at a much lower cost to the environment than cotton. It also grows well in poor quality soil and soaks up carbon dioxide as it does so. Tencel, a fabric that is derived from fast-growing eucalyptus plants, is growing in popularity. Also, orange skins and pineapple leaves, which are waste products left over from the production of fruit juice, can be used. Pineapple leaves, for instance, make a very convincing alternative to leather and a far better one than the 'fake' leather that is usually made from oil-based PVC.

Promoters of **sustainable** fashion also need to widen their appeal by becoming more size-inclusive, by providing plus-sized and petite garments for those who struggle to find clothes that will fit them in high street stores.

1. This chart shows the actual and forecast amounts for spending on clothing in the UK from 2013 until 2026

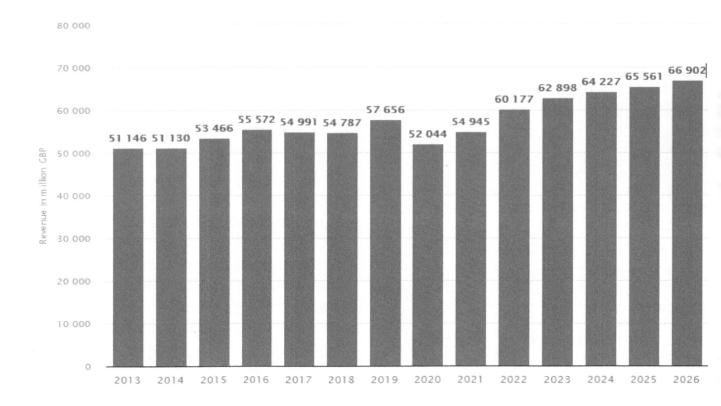

  a. Describe the trends shown.

  b. Can you explain the fall in revenue in 2020-2021?

  c. The forecast for 2026 (£66,902,000,000) amounts to almost £1,000 per person in the UK. Is it necessary to spend so much on what we wear? Why / why not?

2. Carry out an audit of your own wardrobe. What could you do with the clothes that you no longer wear? Could they be repaired, repurposed or recycled?

3. Write a letter to the head of a large fashion house, urging them to adopt a clear policy on recycling unwanted clothing.

Background

While many people have given some thought to what might happen when the world runs out of oil, few seem to have considered what could occur if there wasn't any coffee. This is surprising as coffee is the second most sought-after commodity in the world; the demand far outstrips that for gas, gold, sugar, and corn, for example. Suggestions that the varieties of coffee we know today might be off the menu for good within 20-30 years are not so far-fetched. It is a fragile crop that is affected by the kinds of social, economic, and environmental changes we can see all around us. How would we all cope without our daily caffeine fix?

A brief history of coffee

Legend has it that a monk discovered coffee in Ethiopia during the 13th century. He noticed that, when the goats that he was looking after ate a particular berry, they became restless and overexcited. He reported this to his superiors at the monastery who then created a beverage that kept them awake during late night prayer meetings. Coffee reached Europe in the 17th century and triggered something of a social revolution. Some considered it so controversial that they tried to ban it. Much as they do today, people would gather in coffee houses where, for a penny, they could get their fix of caffeine while engaging in debate and sampling the arts. For this reason, coffee houses also came to be known as 'penny universities'.

Today, 2,250,000,000 or 2.25 billion cups are drunk every day. We estimate that just under 170 million sacks of beans will be exported during 2021, each weighing between 50-70kg. That's around 10 billion (10×10^9) kilos of coffee or 10 million tonnes of it, the same weight as roughly one and a half million elephants, 30,000 jumbo jets or almost a quarter of a million humpback whales. 600-800 million people rely on coffee to make their living, which is 10% of the population of the entire world. We have even built whole countries on it.

Why the alarm?

Yet the alarm bells are already ringing in the coffee industry. Some predict that the total area capable of producing coffee could reduce by up to 88% before 2050. It is not a crop that will tolerate a great deal of environmental change and most of the coffee grown today is one of just two varieties - *arabica* and *robusta*. Both need rich soils, a stable tropical climate and a diverse **ecosystem** that is resistant to pests and disease to thrive. **Climate change** is putting all this at risk. Already, production in some parts of the world is declining because of changes in temperature, lengthy **droughts** and the invasion of pests and fungi. The COVID pandemic has also resulted in a huge backlog of unshipped beans lying on quaysides all over the world, slowing down the economies of those countries that rely on being able to export it. Admittedly, there are some alternatives to these two varieties of coffee, but there we find these only in Ethiopia which has already taken a severe beating from **climate change**.

A world without coffee?

Most of the effects of there being little or no coffee in the world would be negative, but there would be some ways in which the environment would benefit. No longer would the coffee processing industry pollute millions of litres of water every day, which would help to tackle water stress in many parts of the world. There would also be less waste. Each tonne of coffee produced generates twice its weight in discarded husks, although these do make good **fertiliser** and bedding for some pets. You may need to do some explaining to your guinea pig.

The economic effects, however, would be more keenly felt. In high-income countries (HICs) the lack of caffeine would have knock-on effects for all kinds of industries. In the US alone, coffee is worth $45.4 billion every year. Large companies - not only chains of coffee shops, for whom the drink is their main offering, but also the manufacturers of energy drinks, certain drugs and cosmetics - would have to restructure to survive, but they would be unlikely to go bust. It is more likely that Starbucks, for example, would just sell us posh tea or hot chocolate instead, or we would all meet up to drink the latest milkshakes.

In low-income countries, however, the effects would be much more serious. In South America, for example, they predict that up to 25 million farmers would become destitute. Add their dependents and that becomes upwards of 100 million people who would have no income, which would trigger a whole variety of other social and economic problems.

The social effects of the disappearance of coffee would also be very significant. To begin with, many people who relied on it to wake up in the mornings or remain focused during the day would suffer from withdrawal symptoms, becoming moody, irritable and suffering from headaches. It would be as if half the world suddenly started behaving like teenagers who couldn't face going to school. And while they would soon get their fix from other sources, we would have to find other ways of interacting socially. Everything from first dates to meeting up with friends, from catching up on missed lectures to doing multi-million-pound business deals happens over a cup of coffee. So, if you think you might need a new chat-up line in the coming years, now is the time to start thinking. Somehow, 'Do you want to come in for a beer and caramel milkshake?' (which does, incidentally, exist) might mean you remain single for the foreseeable future.

1. This map shows how much coffee is consumed by different countries around the world

Current Worldwide Annual Coffee Consumption per capita

Coffee Consumption
- ☐ Less than 0.8
- ☐ 0.8 – 2.4
- ☐ 2.4 – 4.5
- ■ 4.5 – 6.8
- ■ 6.8 – 12.0
- ☐ No data

Kilograms per person per year

   a. Describe the distribution of coffee consumption around the world

   b. 'Produced by the poor and consumed by the rich.' Is this a fair description of the coffee trade?

2. In what ways would the environment benefit if the production of coffee were to cease worldwide?

3. Do some research into the alternatives to the two main varieties of coffee that we drink now.

   a. What makes them so vulnerable to environmental change?

   b. Would you consider drinking synthetic coffee?

4. A typical coffee break lasts around twenty minutes, whereas the traditional Japanese Tea Ceremony can take up to four hours!

   a. How might people's social lives change in a world without coffee?

   b. What other possibly slower and more prolonged forms of social interaction might we adopt?

Background

Meat is big business. Worldwide, 325 million tonnes of it were produced in 2019 to feed the 73% of the world's population who consider themselves to be **omnivores**. Yet, producing and consuming this much meat is **unsustainable**, partly because of the damage that it does to us when we consume it to excess, but also because of the damage that it does to the environment. In response to this, many people have become vegans. In fact, the number of vegans in the UK has increased by 300% between 2006, when there were around 150,000 and 2018 when there were well over half a million. And, although this diet does not suit all of us, we are all going to have to think more carefully about what we eat because of how it affects both us and the environment.

Why change?

The fact is we only need a fraction of the meat that most of us eat. Experts recommend that we limit ourselves to three servings per week, each of about 100-150g which is roughly the size of a quarter-pound beefburger. However, we would struggle to live without any access to animals and their byproducts (e.g., milk, leather, eggs) at all. Meat is much richer in protein than plants and contains many essential **micronutrients**. Sheep and cows also graze marginal land that is not of much use for anything else. And, looking further afield, we see that in many cultures, livestock are a currency of sorts. The Masai, in Tanzania and Kenya, for example, amass vast herds as signs of their wealth and influence.

Why all the fuss?

Eating too much meat has a few adverse effects. First, there is the effect that eating too much red and processed meat has on our health. Those who eat more than the recommended amount of red meat each week open themselves up to an increased risk of stroke, heart disease, Type 2 Diabetes, and certain types of cancer. They are also more likely to suffer from high levels of cholesterol in their blood and to become obese. Secondly, there are the animals themselves, whose health and welfare are often the last thing on the minds of those who simply want to fatten them up and kill them. Then there is the effect on the environment. The meat industry contributes both directly and indirectly to **deforestation**, causes vast amounts of **greenhouse gases** such as carbon dioxide, methane, and nitrous oxide to be released into the atmosphere and wrecks the soil. It also uses vast amounts of water. To produce a single gram of beef uses 112 litres of H_2O, which means that it takes roughly 11,200 litres to produce a single quarter pounder. That's enough to have a five-minute shower every day of the week for about four months.

What are the alternatives?

There are two ways in which you could eat less meat and still have a perfectly adequate diet. One way would be to become a vegetarian or a vegan. This has many benefits: you are less likely to be overweight, your blood pressure is likely to be lower than your meat-eating friend's and you are likely to be, generally, healthier than they are. On the other hand, you are likely to find that your choices are quite limited when eating out, although there are signs that this is improving with many restaurants and supermarkets offering plant-based alternatives to meat. You will also need to think much more carefully about what you eat in order to make sure that your diet is balanced, and you may need to take some dietary supplements, but these are easily found in chemists and health food shops.

Another strategy is to eat meat alternatives. This could be food that is made to taste like meat but is, in fact, either plant-based or synthetic. Algae is already being farmed on a massive scale off the coast of New Mexico for example where it is turned into protein shakes and bars among other things. And chicken nuggets, grown in a laboratory, that contain no meat - at least not as we know it - are not far away.

Another food possible source of protein is eating insects to consume the amounts of protein that are needed for a healthy diet. Those who are in favour of this point out that they are both good for us and for the environment. Indeed, it has been estimated that as many as 1,000 different species of insects might be edible. Also, although it may seem gross and remind you of celebrities eating maggots on live television, bugs already make up part of the diet of over 2 billion people. A few grams of protein derived from crickets each day, for example, could compensate for much of what is missing from the diets of people in Asia and Africa and be a very powerful weapon in the face of malnutrition. Bugs also give off almost no **greenhouse gases** whatsoever. For example, a gram of protein produced by farming crickets gives off only 0.1% or one-thousandth of the methane that a cow produces producing the same amount of meat. And the trouble doesn't seem to be that they taste disgusting … rather that they are very bland and taste of almost nothing at all.

1. This graph predicts the volumes of conventional, cultured (i.e., grown in a laboratory) and meat substitutes (i.e., derived from plants) that will be sold from 2025 until 2040.

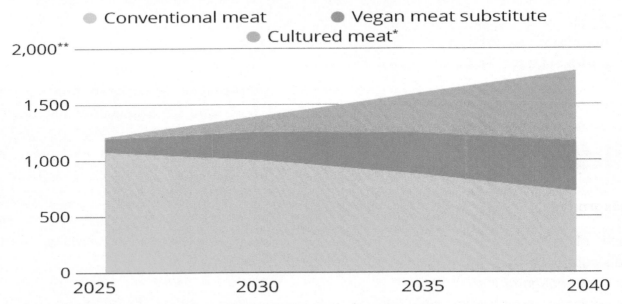

New Meat for the World

Global sales of traditional meat and meat worldwide in billion U.S. dollars from 2025 to 2040

● Conventional meat   ● Vegan meat substitute
● Cultured meat*

* Meat produced in the laboratory by tissue engineering
** Numbers are rounded to hundred billions
Source: Kearney

a. Describe the trends that you see above.

b. Do you think that the demand for 'real' meat will decline as sharply as the graph suggests? Explain your answer.

c. What do you suppose you will be eating in the 2050s? Will you become a vegan or vegetarian (assuming that you are not one already) relying on pulses, fruit, vegetables, and dietary supplements? Will you opt for non-conventional meat products or, perhaps, resort to eating grasshoppers?

Background

Much of the rich world has a love-hate relationship with food. On the one hand, we can't get enough of it or get it quickly enough. For example, worldwide obesity has tripled since 1975 and there are currently almost two billion overweight people globally. Today, ready meals are part of the diet of 88% of people in the UK, with 40% eating them at least once a week. On the other hand, most of us who live in High-Income Countries (HICs) throw away our own weight in food waste every three months, most of which is perfectly edible.

What's wrong with our attitude to food?

We are making lots of bad choices about what we eat. Not only do many of us choose diets that are too high in salt, sugar and fat, but we seem to care very little about how our food gets to us and what happens to the food that we don't end up eating.

To begin with, we don't seem to care much about how our food is produced, growing tomatoes all year round in heated greenhouses without thinking about the consequences; and chowing down on beefburgers while cattle fill the atmosphere with methane. We spray the fields with **fertiliser**s to increase crop yields then stand and watch as the intense rainfall washes it all off the fields into our rivers and oceans.

Admittedly, it has been fashionable in recent years to draw attention to the distance that our food has travelled to reach our plates. We know that food that crosses the oceans, whether it is exotic fruit from the tropics or meat from the other side of the world, is very expensive to transport. This is especially so when perishable food travels as air freight. This can be up to fifty times more expensive than shipping and accounts for 11% of all **greenhouse gases** given off by UK food transport. Even when it has reached our shores, moving food around the UK is costly. 25% of all the heavy goods vehicles (HGVs) on our roads are moving food around and releasing 1.9 million tonnes of CO_2 into the atmosphere in the process. Then there are our journeys to the supermarket to fill up our trolleys - another 135 miles per person per year.

Yet, this is only a small part of the problem, a far greater one being the amount of food waste that we create. Food waste is defined as "any removal of food from the **food chain** which is or was at some point fit for human consumption or which has spoiled or expired". Some of this waste takes place before it even reaches the consumer with crops getting damaged during harvesting, or being stored, packed, or transported incorrectly. Then, up to 50% of the harvest can get rejected because it does not meet food standards about size, shape, weight or colour. Finally, we make wrong decisions about whether food has "gone off" and throw it away unnecessarily. In the UK alone, 50 million chickens and 100 million pints of milk go to waste every year.

Taking Action

In the light of all the miles that our food travels, it might seem wise to stop importing food altogether. However, this would have little effect on emissions of **greenhouse gases**, which might only fall by as little as 0.1% as a result. There are also the livelihoods of the people elsewhere in the world who rely on exporting food to the UK to consider as there are 1.5 million of them in sub-Saharan Africa alone.

One way forward is to be more accepting of food that doesn't "make the grade" or which goes unsold. UK supermarkets have begun to do this in recent years, offering underweight and misshapen produce to consumers at reduced prices rather than destroy them. Cafes, supermarkets, and restaurants increasingly make their leftover produce available to local charities at the end of the day, something which has recently become the law in France. We should also consider eating more methodically. This can be something as simple as making a meal plan or going to the supermarket with a list rather than wandering aimlessly along the aisles and being hooked by every special offer that is going. If we buy food nearby that is in season, we will reduce the need for refrigerated storage while also supporting local producers. We will then need less food to be air freighted to us and will benefit from the many vitamins and minerals that are lost when food must be frozen or stored over long periods of time. Even being a little wiser with our leftovers can help, whether that means stripping a chicken carcass for meat to make a pie or a curry so that you get two meals out of one bird or by building a compost heap in your garden to recycle organic waste.

Another very effective thing that we can do is reduce the amount of meat and dairy products in our diets. Not only is this good for our health, but it also means that, in the long term, land that was used for livestock could either be used to produce crops, which give a far greater return in terms of calories per m^2 or returned to its natural state. One estimate suggests that, if it were possible to divert all the grain that is currently grown to feed cattle to feed people instead, up to four billion more people need not go hungry.

1. Look at these figures about food waste in different parts of the world

	North America	Europe	Sub-Saharan Africa
Pre-consumer waste (kg/person/yr)	185	190	155
Post-consumer waste (kg/person/yr)	110	90	5
Total waste	295	280	160

    a. Present this data as either a divided bar graph or as a series of proportional circles where the area of the circle relates to the total amount of food wasted.

    b. Can you explain the marked differences between the amount of food wasted in different parts of the world and the way(s) in which it is wasted?

2. "The less food travels, the better." To what extent do you agree? Give reasons.

Background

With the world's population approaching 7.9 billion (2021), and the current number of cars on the road being around 1.4 billion, there is currently roughly one car for every 5.5 people on Earth. Currently, of these 1,400,000,000 vehicles, a massive 98% run on either petrol or diesel. That leaves just 28,000,000 cars running on electricity, **biofuel**, hydrogen cells or solar power, roughly one for every person who lives in Madagascar (27.6 million in 2020). Meanwhile, all the vehicles that run on petrol or diesel are pumping out 2.23 billion tonnes of CO_2 into the atmosphere every year. That's 1.6 tonnes per car, or over twenty times the weight of the average person, which is roughly 67kg according to researchers at the London School of Hygiene and Tropical Medicine.

So, what are our options?

Now that the UK government has set some of the most challenging targets for reducing emissions in the whole world (an 80% reduction in CO_2 emissions by 2050), the race is on to replace the 31.7 million cars that we drive with more environmentally friendly alternatives. The main contender is the electric vehicle (EV) of which there are just over a quarter of a million on the roads as of June 2021. In addition to this, there are also plans to introduce cars that run on **biofuels**, solar power, and hydrogen, although these are still at an experimental stage.

Electric Vehicles

Cars that run exclusively on electricity are still relatively few, but hybrid models have become increasingly popular in recent years. In a hybrid car, an electric motor and a petrol engine work together to provide the power for the car. This contributes to better fuel economy (i.e., more miles for every tank of petrol) and reduces carbon emissions. However, a car that runs exclusively on green energy is even better for the environment as this reduces its **carbon footprint** to practically zero. Advantages of investing in an electric car include government-backed incentive schemes which reduce the upfront cost of buying the vehicle to little more than the cost of a traditional petrol-powered vehicle. Electric cars are also less expensive to run. A full overnight charge, when electricity tends to be cheaper anyway, costs around £4.00, which is about 10% of the cost of a full tank of petrol. Furthermore, there is also a growing network of charging points around the country.

On the other hand, electric cars are not for everyone. They may be quiet and comfortable as the suspension must be good enough to carry the heavy battery, but many drivers and passengers find the silence unnerving. Some campaigners have argued for them to have speakers installed to make them sound like 'normal' cars for reasons of road safety. Other issues of concern include poor access to domestic charging points as 40% of the UK population lives in rented accommodation and 20% live in flats. Added to this, there is range anxiety, which is when drivers worry about their batteries going flat before they reach their destination or about not being able to recharge their vehicles once there. Finally, electric cars tend to be around £10,000 more expensive than their petrol and diesel-fueled equivalents.

Biofuels

Biofuels, which are fuels made by fermenting plants or waste products with significant amounts of sugar in them, are another option. Already small amounts are mixed with petrol and diesel to improve fuel efficiency and reduce emissions of carbon monoxide (CO) and sulphur dioxide (SO_2). For example, the ethanol content of standard grade petrol in the UK was recently doubled from 5% (E5) to 10% of the total mix (E10). Supporters of **biofuels** argue that they combat **climate change** as, while they grow, the plants absorb CO_2 from the atmosphere. Growing plants to make **biofuels** creates jobs, too. However, large areas of land that might otherwise be used to grow food are used to grow **biofuels** and these, in turn, require large quantities of water and **fertiliser**. The oils used in the process might also be sourced from the rainforests and this implies reduced **biodiversity** and loss of **habitat**.

Solar-powered cars and hydrogen fuel cells

Two other possibilities are solar and hydrogen-powered vehicles. In 2020, a two-seat, three-wheel solar-powered car was launched which, for $26,000 (c. £19,000) would travel up to 50 miles if left to charge in full sunlight for up to six hours. This would be fine if you happened to work in the desert in California but would fare less well if parked in a multi-story car park in Central London. Cars fueled by hydrogen are also being developed. These have the massive advantage that the only waste product they produce is water. However, there is almost nowhere where you can refuel them at present and they are very expensive in the first place.

6.5 Things to do

1. Draft a letter to the transport minister, recommending and justifying a strategy for phasing out vehicles that run on petrol and diesel.

2. One significant problem with electric vehicles is that there are few places to charge them. How would you go about solving this problem?

3. To what extent do you agree with the statement that increasing the use of biofuels creates more problems than it solves.

Background

Energy. Without it, we wouldn't be going anywhere or doing anything at all. Yet, if current trends continue, we will soon reach a point where we cannot find the energy we need at a price that we can afford to pursue our frankly, rather wasteful lifestyles. We are going to have to look for it in other places or, which is preferable, stop demanding so much of it in the first place.

A looming crisis

There are plenty of reasons to suggest that we might be heading for an energy crisis. First, the energy sources that we have relied upon to power our factories and homes are running low. The world gets through 40,000 gallons of oil (180,000 litres) every single second. If it were sold in barrels the size of Olympic swimming pools, we would drain one every 3.5 seconds. Estimates as to when the three main fossil fuels - oil, coal and natural gas - will run out vary but fifty years for oil and gas and about 110 years for coal are reasonable estimates. This is partly because the world's population is still growing rapidly. As many newly emerging economies continue to

develop, their energy use per capita also increases. For example, between 2009 and 2019 the average person in China went from consuming 19,902 kWh to 27,452 kWh per annum, an increase of 38%. The problem is made worse by an almost complete lack of interest in **sustainable** alternatives. Even now, the amount of energy generated from renewable sources is only around 5%.

Where are we heading?

Thankfully, we are starting to fall out of love with fossil fuels. We have finally realised that they will not last forever and that they do tremendous damage the environment. But when supplies of anything start to run out and there are few viable alternatives on offer. several things can happen. First, the price starts to rise. This affects us personally, as we can see it each time we visit a petrol station or get a gas or electricity bill. But it also affects the economy. For example, practically all industries currently rely on oil in the form of petrol to generate the power that they need and to transport their goods around the world. Many, however, also use it as a raw material, so some of the less obvious consequences of a world oil shortage might include more expensive cosmetics, food, clothes, medication, plastics and even cars. This could lead to large numbers of jobs being lost in these industries.

Why the urgency?

If we fail to tackle the energy crisis then energy insecurity becomes a serious issue. This is when a country can no longer secure a reliable and affordable supply of energy to meet its needs. If this happens and demand cannot be reduced, energy will either have to be rationed or people will have to start looking for it in ever more sensitive and inaccessible places. If we chose the rationing option, both our home lives and our workplaces would be affected. And while a power cut in the middle of an episode of *EastEnders* might be a nuisance, having to shut a factory down for several hours a day would have far more serious consequences.

If, instead, we decided to widen our search for energy and venture into places like the rainforest and the Arctic tundra we risk damaging them irreparably. If it involves asking other countries to provide the energy we need or even to allow it to cross their borders, politics comes into play, and this could lead to increased tension between countries or even real conflict.

What can be done?

Possibly the most important thing to do to tackle the energy crisis is to educate people to make more **sustainable** choices. In the long term, it may be possible to find alternatives to fossil fuels that will deliver all our energy needs but this time will be many years in the future. People need to understand the need for energy efficiency so that it changes both their spending habits and their behaviour, from how they travel to which light bulbs they buy and how much energy their washing machine uses. There need to be ways in which people can get credit for putting energy into the system and not just bills for taking it out. This already happens in some small way using solar panels, but further innovation is needed here. For example, in China, you can be paid for recycling your plastic and, in Russia, a few minutes on a treadmill at the entrance to the subway will earn you a discount on your fare. Exploiting solar power in countries where there are sufficient hours of sunlight is another way forward. Already solar panels are being integrated into buildings to provide power without the need for a mains connection; there is even the prospect of huge floating solar panels out at sea.

What are the obstacles?

Whichever of these options we choose, however, there are going to be obstacles along the way. Some of the biggest companies and richest people in the world, for example, have built their fortunes on oil. They will do everything in their power to make sure that their profits are not hit by a move to renewable energy sources. They will also use their influence to try to dissuade governments from signing up to any agreements that are not in their interests. Finally, there is the question of whether we can persuade people to change their habits so radically. After all, who wants their view spoiled by a huge wind farm or will hand over the keys to their 4x4 in exchange for a free bus pass?

1. This chart shows how the amount of energy generated from renewable sources has changed over recent years in the United Kingdom.

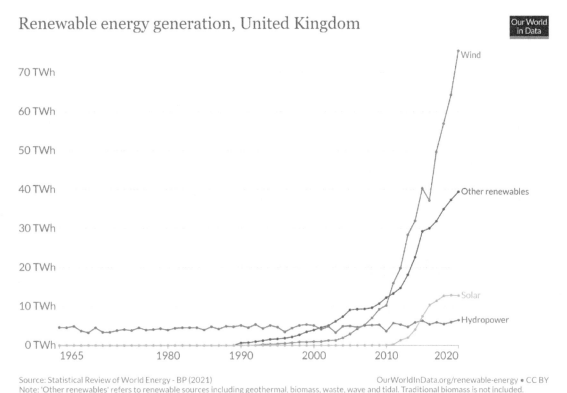

Renewable energy generation, United Kingdom

Source: Statistical Review of World Energy - BP (2021)   OurWorldInData.org/renewable-energy • CC BY
Note: 'Other renewables' refers to renewable sources including geothermal, biomass, waste, wave and tidal. Traditional biomass is not included.

    a. Describe the pattern that you see.

    b. Can you explain…

        i.   Why wind power proved so popular?

        ii.   Why the contribution of solar power seems to have reached a plateau?

        iii.   Why the contribution of hydropower not changed much in 50 years?

2. Use them less or find some more? Which approach do you favour when it comes to fossil fuels?

3. Would you accept a free lifetime pass to use public transport in exchange for promising never to travel in a car again?

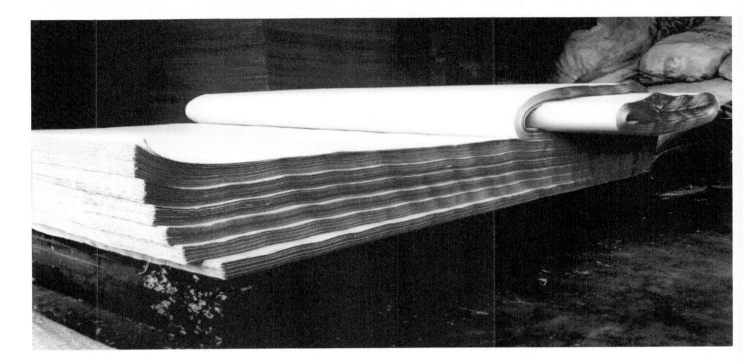

Background

Paper is everywhere. We write on it, use it to make disposable plates and cutlery, wipe things with it, blow our noses on it ... the list is almost endless. In the USA alone, 68 million trees are felled annually to make paper. That's roughly one tree for every five people in the country. Meanwhile, in the UK, we get through 12,500,000 tonnes of the stuff annually. This is about 200kg for every single person in the UK ... or, put another way, three times their weight. What is more, 12% of all the energy used for manufacturing is used to make paper, all of which helped make the paper and pulp industry the fourth-largest emitter of **greenhouse gases** in 2007. Finally, when we have finished with it, we fail to recycle it, sending it instead to be buried in landfill sites where it makes up 25% of all buried waste and rots away, giving off methane. Neither is the situation getting better. It was not so long ago that dreams of a paperless society looked like they might come true. But it simply isn't happening; in fact, demand for paper is predicted to double by the year 2030.

Ending our love affair with paper

There are plenty of reasons why we need to cut down on our use of paper. First, although much of the world's paper is produced from **sustainable** sources, 75% of the plantations established since 2000 have been at the expense of natural forests. The paper industry depletes water supplies and pollutes them with chemicals as well as threatening **habitats** and driving away animals due to the noise. Elephants, leopards, chimpanzees, and pandas are among those threatened in this way. Trees also detoxify the air, so a reduction in their number will worsen air quality. Their absence also leads to increased soil erosion as the ground is exposed to the baking heat of the sun, dries up and is blown away or is carried off in flash-flooding events. Finally, without their roots to hold the soil together, landslides and mudslides are becoming more and more common.

How would we benefit?

Cutting down on the amount of paper we use would have many benefits on top of those we would enjoy from leaving the forest alone. First, it would decrease our use of other resources: less paper would mean less ink, fewer printers, staples, and Tippex. It would also cut our energy bills. Recycling paper is up to 70% more energy-efficient than creating it from scratch, so we can even make a difference without having to sacrifice our tissues, newspapers, and notebooks. Using less paper could also mean that schools and offices could make better use of space as rooms that were once full of archived materials could be given over other uses. They could also be more efficient. This is because, while a society that prints everything can only let one person at a time refer to a document at once, many people can refer to an electronic document at the same time.

How can this be achieved?

There are many things for which we use paper where alternatives would not be difficult to find. It has already been mentioned that the electronic storage of information would cut down on its use and tablets, computers and smartphones make this more and more possible. However, we must be wary of the activities of cybercriminals if our data is not to be stolen or held to ransom by our competitors and even our enemies. Items such as toilet rolls and tissues that are currently made from paper can be made from fast-growing bamboo and kitchen roll can be replaced with microfibre cloths that can be washed after use. Furthermore, for every tonne of paper that we recycle, we can save 7,000 gallons of water,

meaning that roughly every 100 tonnes of paper recycled saves enough water to fill an Olympic-sized swimming pool.

Another strategy that could have a very significant impact would be to do away with disposable cups, which are responsible for the felling of 6,500,000 trees every year. Sixteen billion cups, or more than two for every person on the planet, are thrown away annually. And, because they are coated in plastic to stop the liquid just soaking through the paper and giving you soggy hands, they can't be recycled. Better to have your very own reusable cup which you take along to Starbucks each morning and put through your dishwasher when you get home from work. Cutting down on packaging is another area where easy gains can be made. Wrapping our parcels and presents in plain brown paper rather than glossy paper would allow the paper to be recycled. Finally, we can promote hot-desking at work as people are far less likely to allow piles of paper to build up in their offices if desks have to be cleared for other colleagues to work at later in the day.

1. This chart shows how much paper and paperboard has been used globally since 1992

Global paper and paperboard market, million metric tons

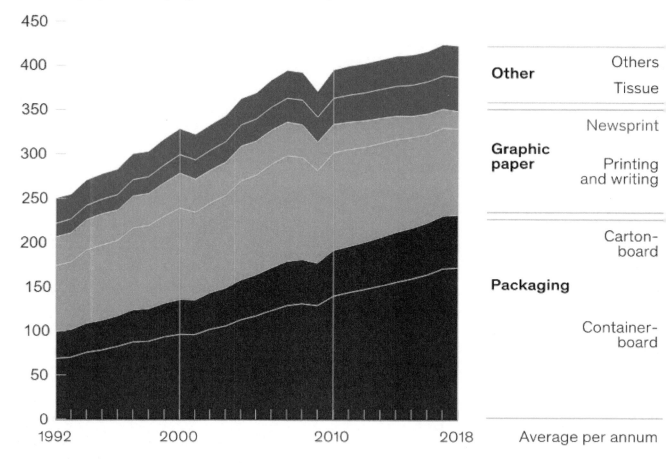

a. What has fueled the increased demand for paper and paperboard?

b. What hope do you think there is of a paperless or paper-light society in the foreseeable future? Give your reasons.

c. What ways of minimising your own use of paper are achievable and realistic?

d. Design a poster to persuade customers at your local cafe to bring in their own cups and mugs.

e. Start a campaign in your school to minimise the use and wastage of paper.

Background

"Space", as Douglas Adams observed in *The Hitchhikers' Guide to the Galaxy*, "is big ....". "You just won't believe how vastly, hugely, mind-bogglingly big it is", he continues. And there are more than a few things flying around in it. Tons of debris, for example, orbit around the earth, nearly all of which we put up there by launching rockets and satellites. And it's getting quite crowded, as suggested in the film *Gravity*. What concerns us more than the bits of junk that we put there in the first place, however, are meteors; lumps of rock of various sizes that orbit the sun in much the same way as the Earth does. This is because there is a possibility, however small, that they might collide with the Earth with devastating consequences.

What are the chances?

In the short term, NASA assures us we are safe. It is unlikely that a meteor capable of ending civilisation, i.e., exceeding one km in diameter, is going to strike before the end of the 21st century. Smaller rocks enter our atmosphere regularly. Rocks less than 5 m across are an annual event, but they strike unpopulated areas or burn up in the atmosphere. Larger examples have caused significant damage in recent years, most recently near Chelyabinsk in Russia in 2013, where a specimen estimated to weigh 10,000 tonnes and travelling at 40,000 miles per hour injured about 1,500 people. The most recent meteor big enough to threaten civilisation created the Gulf of Mexico 66 million years ago.

What would happen?

If another meteor of that size were to hit Earth, our chances of survival would be low but, for some people who were in the right place at the right time, survival could be possible. The most significant effect would be the ash from the fires and debris from the impact. These would completely block out the sunlight for as much as two years after the event. This would reduce global temperatures by 50°F (28°C) so that the only tropics would remain above freezing. The fires would also cover the soil in a mixture of ash and molten rock, along with a thick clay crust. This would make them **infertile**, and any water that ran off into the oceans would make them highly acidic and harmful to marine life.

The absence of any significant sunlight would also bring photosynthesis to a halt so that nothing that depended upon it could grow. Rainfall, much of which is caused by **convection** currents that are driven by the sun, would also reduce considerably. It would snow continuously in some places for many years.

The ability to manufacture anything would also be very limited as we would lose all the gains made in the agricultural and industrial revolutions and much of the **infrastructure** that held up society.

Can we do anything?

There is not much that we can do to prevent the cataclysmic consequences of a potential "earth killer" for those who remain on the surface, save trying to deflect the offending rock with explosives. **Earth killers** are those meteors that NASA thinks might collide with the Earth in the future, which are also over one kilometre across. But, while they think they have spotted most of the culprits, they could still miss smaller lumps of rock capable of doing some serious damage. Prediction, therefore, will only alarm the majority.

Preparation, however, could be worthwhile if only to sustain the relatively small numbers of people who could be protected from the initial blast. It would be wise to build up stocks of food for the many years during which harvests would be close to non-existent, to dig extensive networks of underground tunnels where the privileged few could ride out both the extreme heat of the impact itself and the cold of the "impact winter" that followed, and to put by seeds capable of growing in low light conditions. Planting trees would be a wise move as they have ways of surviving at extremes, as would learning to love mushrooms and other fungi that can grow in the dark.

The areas in which humans would have any realistic chance of surviving on the surface are limited. They would have to be well above sea level to avoid being swamped by tsunami waves and relatively close to the tropics, as this would be the only place where there was liquid water. A camp beside the upper reaches of a river on a tropical island might be a good bet as the river would supply you with water and, perhaps, a little food and a way of getting out to sea. Or you could venture deep into a cave for shelter from the extremes of temperature. One thing is for certain, you would have to get used to eating a completely different diet, including the six years' worth of tinned and dried food that you would have had to put aside. And as for your sources of protein, these would be limited to a few types of insects as, with no grass growing anywhere, grazing animals such as sheep and cows would not survive for long. If you were lucky, you might breed a few rather scrawny pigs for the occasional sausage or resort to eating more unusual creatures. A recipe book from Mauritius, which would be an ideal place to ride out the storm, says that hedgehogs taste good.

1. The graph below shows the Torino Scale, used to decide how much of a threat a particular near-Earth object is likely to be. The scale goes from 0 (nothing to worry about at all) to 10 (a certain collision capable of destroying all of civilisation)

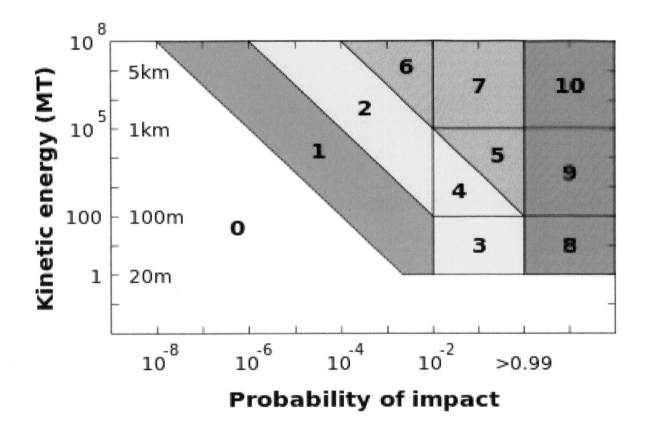

1. Both the x and y-axes are peculiar. What is unusual about them?

2. All events involving meteors under 20 metres in diameter are deemed to be not worth worrying about. Do you agree with this judgement?

2. "When we can't save everyone, we should save nobody." Do you agree? Explain your answer.

3. Imagine that it is 2050. You have a young family and have been given notice that a meteor that is 5 km wide will certainly strike Central Europe in five years. What will you do?

Background

While many of the threats to our continued existence come from elsewhere in the universe, for example, meteor strikes, solar flares and alien invasion, there is one that comes from within the earth itself, which is the threat of another super-volcanic eruption. A super-volcano, which was a term first used not by geologists but by a travel writer in the 1920s, are those volcanoes that can throw over 1,000 km^3 of material into the atmosphere and which are categorised as 8 or above on the Volcanic Explosivity Index (VEI). This is a mind-boggling large quantity of rock, molten rock and ash; even the eruption of Mount Saint Helens in the USA only managed 2 km^3. There has not been such an eruption for tens of thousands of years.

Where are these super-volcanoes and what are they like?

Super-volcanoes are quite unlike what we might call 'normal' volcanoes, which we think of as being shaped like mountains. Imagine a massive egg frying upside down in a pan about 100 kilometres wide and you begin to get the idea. This shape is because it has ejected such an enormous amount of molten rock from below the surface that the crust has collapsed into the empty space, forming a **caldera**. Such landforms are hard to spot at ground level because they are so huge and because there are so few clues on the surface. We know of about twenty such landforms, including super-volcanoes in California, Japan, Indonesia, Italy, New Zealand, Chile and possibly Alaska. They can form over hot spots in the Earth's **mantle**, forming chains of volcanoes as **convection** currents drag tectonic plates over them. This is how we think the Hawaiian Islands were formed. We can also find them along destructive plate boundaries where there are vast amounts of molten rock trapped below the surface because of oceanic crust sinking deep into the Earth. One such **reservoir** lies deep below the Andes mountains in South America.

What would an eruption be like?

The geological record, which is the story that rocks can tell us, suggests that a super-volcanic eruption could well be fatal for a large part of civilisation. In 1815, the eruption of Tambora threw material over 28,000 metres into the atmosphere, which is over three times the height of Mt Everest. An avalanche of super-heated rock and ash followed, burying a wide area with ash over 30 centimetres deep. With the sun blocked out and the soils rendered **infertile**, over 82,000 people died of starvation in the two years which followed. In the event of a super-volcanic eruption, the United Nations has forecast that we would exhaust food supplies in a little over two months. Other consequences might include a reduction in global temperatures of up to 5°C as sulphur dioxide would fill the atmosphere. Geologists have predicted that if the eruption was to take place in Yellowstone National Park in the USA, the initial shock would kill upwards of 90,000 people incinerating everything within a radius of 60 miles. Almost continuous earthquakes would rock the entire area for many months, while clouds of dense, hot ash would travel outwards from the site of the eruption at around 30-40 miles per hour. Those that survived the initial blast would inevitably suffer from respiratory problems. If the eruption occurred on or near the coast, there would also be the possibility of a tsunami wave to contend with.

So, we're doomed, then?

Well, yes and no. We can derive some reassurance from the fact that every one of the twenty potential super-volcanoes is being carefully monitored by scientists from all over the world. However, there is no evidence that these events happen at regular intervals, so we can't make accurate forecasts from past geological activity. They simply don't follow a pattern. There has not been an eruption that would reach VEI 9 or above in 10,000 years and, taking Yellowstone as an example, there would have to be far greater quantities of molten lava beneath the surface than there are at present to exert the required pressure to cause a catastrophic eruption. Geologists have even suggested that we could prevent an eruption and that the magma chamber beneath Yellowstone, for example, might, ultimately, be tamed and its heat used to generate **geothermal** power. The idea would be to drill down into the earth's surface near the magma chamber and fill the wells that were created with water turning Yellowstone National Park into a giant **geothermal** energy plant. This would cause some of the molten rock beneath the surface to cool and solidify so that it no longer put pressure on the rocks above it. There are many problems with this approach, however. First, it would take a vast quantity of water, electricity, and time in an area where it is in short supply to have any effect on the temperature of the molten rock; some suggest that the magma chamber would not cool sufficiently for as long as 16,000 years. Also, the project would risk causing precisely the eruption that it seeks to avoid. This is because boreholes, drilled into the rock, might weaken it and make it unable to contain the magma within.

One thing we can do, however, is to make some preparations. It is unlikely that such an eruption would arrive unannounced, so there is time to stockpile food and water in areas where there is little tectonic activity. We would also do well to get used to a diet of insects, mushrooms, and bacteria, which might be the only food sources available to us in a significantly dimmed world.

1.   What are the criteria for a super-volcanic eruption?

2.   Look at this map, which shows the distribution of the world's deadliest volcanoes (VEI 7+)

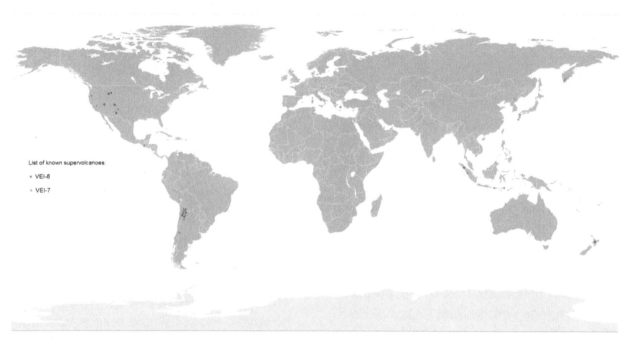

List of known supervolcanoes:

• VEI-8

• VEI-7

   a.   Describe the location of these volcanoes.

   b.   Find a map of major plate boundaries in an atlas. Do all the volcanoes 'match-up' with plate boundaries? What does this suggest?

3.   "We should harness supervolcanoes for their potential to provide geothermal energy." Discuss.

Background

The idea that humans might, at some point, have to leave the Earth, has long been a theme in science fiction and fantasy stories. Among other things, such possibilities inspired the writers of *Star Trek* to send people on imaginary missions to "seek out new life and new civilisations [and] to boldly go where no man had gone before." More recently, however, space scientists and other notable figures have suggested that looking for somewhere else to live - perhaps on another planet or moon within our own solar system, or on a world many light-years away - might not be a waste of time, after all.

What's all the panic?

Professor Stephen Hawking was one of the most outspoken people to suggest that Earth has a very short life expectancy. He said that humanity had no more than 200 years left to establish itself in space before life on Earth descended into chaos. Hawking predicted an increase in crises and conflicts of various kinds

mainly for two main reasons. First, there would be too many people and too few resources; the World Wildlife Fund (WWF) predicts we will need a second planet to meet our demand for resources by 2030. Second, there would be an environmental catastrophe triggered by **climate change**. Other commentators have noted that extinction is a normal thing. Over 99% of the species that have ever lived are now extinct, so to imagine a world that was dominated by some other life form in the future is not as far-fetched as it seems. Others have raised the possibility that we might fall victim to a virus, either of our own creation or from beyond the Earth. Perhaps **artificial intelligence** might turn against us. This is a theme that is explored in the film, *I, Robot*, based on the works of Isaac Asimov.

In contrast, others have more conservative views. For example, while very few of the possible scenarios for the future warming of the planet make for comfortable reading, none of them implies that the Earth will become uninhabitable or that we will simply fry like ants under a magnifying glass. There is no threat to our safety from passing meteorites for many thousands and possibly millions of years and even the most serious epidemics have not come close to wiping out humanity. Suggestions that the world population will continue to grow inexorably are also ill-founded as, already, many high-income countries have fertility rates well below replacement level (e.g., USA, Japan) and low-income countries are starting to follow suit. What is thought most likely is that it will peak at around 11 billion in 2100 and then start to fall.

Reasons for exploring space

Apart from finding somewhere else to live in the event of the Earth not being able to support the growing population, venturing into space has other benefits. Some space scientists have suggested harvesting asteroids for their resources. Many are known to contain ice, which could provide hydrogen for fuel and oxygen to make the air breathable. This would make them potential 'cosmic petrol stations'. Precious metals and raw materials could be brought back to Earth or heavy, polluting industries farmed out to other worlds so that the Earth could be set aside for residential use only. Keeping an eye on what is happening in space could also alert us to hostile forms of life that might prove dangerous to us, although these are more likely to be microscopic bacteria than little green men with three eyes.

Could it really happen?

Some limited steps towards opening up space to the masses are already taking place, though most have only reached the edge of the atmosphere. Space elevators that are capable of pulling massive payloads into space are a real possibility within the next 10-15 years. Huge gondolas travelling along cables some 30-40 miles in length would drag resources beyond Earth's gravitational field, where launching them out into the far reaches of the solar system might be more feasible. Plans are already being made to return to the moon and set up a permanent base there.

However, there are also many obstacles for which no solutions have yet been found. It costs many millions of pounds to put a satellite that is a little bigger than a family car into orbit, so getting sufficient resources even as far as the moon to set up a permanent base there would be ridiculously expensive. Whether we can sustain life beyond the stars is also questionable. We already know that living in a low gravity environment is bad news for our muscles, which tend to waste away when we experience near-weightlessness. People who have spent a long time in space or who have taken part in experiments designed to simulate lengthy journeys across the solar system have also found that it plays havoc with their sleep cycles and body rhythms. The main obstacle to travel to distant galaxies, however, is the mind-boggling distances involved. Even travelling at the highest speeds that rockets can sustain, it would take over 50,000 years to get to the nearest star. This would mean that, if you set off now, your Great x 2.0 x 10^3 grandmother might set foot on Kepler 62E in the year 52,021. Provided, of course, that she didn't mind living almost exclusively on kale and potatoes, which are known to grow well where there is little light, ... and on her own excrement. Yum!

1. This chart shows how much of their GDP a number of countries allocate to their 'space budget' and how much this changed between 2010 and 2015

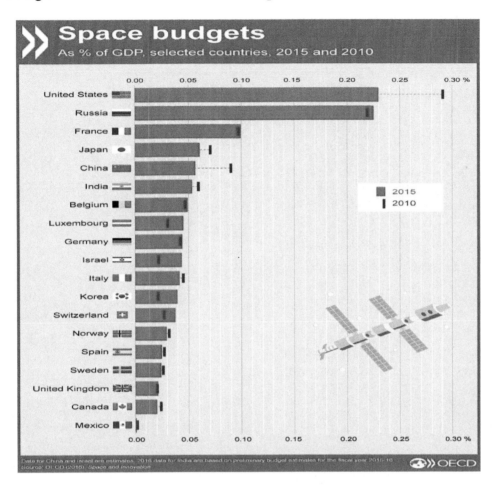

a. Are you surprised by the presence or absence of any country in the list?

b. "Space exploration is a waste of money." Discuss.

2.

a. Do you think there will ever come a time when people will need to migrate into space permanently?

b. If it does come, how should we decide

    i.   Who should go?

    ii.   Where they should be sent?

Background

There is currently about 20,000,000 km³ of ice on Earth. Most of it is locked up in the vast ice sheets that cover Greenland and Antarctica; the rest is trapped in **glaciers**, giant 'rivers' of ice that can be found mainly in the Himalayas and on the west coast of North and South America. Twenty million cubic kilometres might sound like a lot, but it is only about 0.1% of the volume of the moon.

Predictions about when the last **glacier**s and ice sheets might finally disappear completely vary wildly, with some suggesting that 80-90% could have melted by 2050. Others say that it could be another 5000 years before the last of the ice will melt in Antarctica. Scientists measure the amount of ice that melts in gigatons per year or gt/yr.

A gigaton is 1,000 billion tonnes, or 1 x 10¹² tonnes. Between 2000 and 2018, the rate of loss accelerated dramatically as can be seen below:

Period	2000-2004	2005-2009	2010-2014	2015-2018	2000-2018
Glacial melt rate (gt/yr)	227	257	284	292	264

So, what's the damage?

Were all the world's **glaciers** to melt, sea levels could rise by as much as seventy metres, roughly equivalent to the height of a thirty-story block of flats. One estimate suggests that enough ice already melts annually to fill a swimming pool the size of England to a depth of well over 1.5 metres. Major cities, including London, and even entire countries such as Bangladesh and the Maldives could disappear beneath the waves if this were to happen and outlines of countries on the world map would change, possibly quite significantly. Much of South-East England, for example, would be submerged with only the North and South Downs and the High Weald looking out over the much wider English Channel. Florida, along with Rio de Janeiro and its world-famous beaches would disappear completely.

Flooding on this scale could trigger the mass migration of many millions of **refugees**, people who have been forced to move from their homes because of the rising water. There may be as many as half a billion people affected in this way, although it has also been pointed out that they might equally choose to stay put and hold out against the advancing water by building coastal defences or even raising their homes on stilts.

People living in the Andes and the Himalayas would also suffer if **glaciers** started retreating rapidly. It is claimed by some that, even if the whole world were to become **carbon-neutral** by 2050, one-third of the **glaciers** in the Himalayas would already have disappeared and, with them, much of the water that the 1.9 billion people living on the Indian subcontinent need for drinking, energy, and **agriculture**.

Another significant impact would be on the Gulf Stream, a giant conveyor belt of sorts that moves 20 million m^3 of water every second along the east coast of North America from the Gulf of Mexico towards Northern Europe. Relatively warm water, which is lighter than cold water, starts its journey northwards from the tropics, cooling and becoming denser as it does so. Once it reaches the North Atlantic, the current switches direction, the cooler, denser water sinking to the ocean floor and travelling south again. Among other things, this current stops the temperature in Florida and the UK from getting too extreme and affects the intensity and direction of hurricanes in the North Atlantic. If the Gulf Stream were to weaken significantly, winters in the UK and North America would be much colder with more frequent and more severe storms. This was the premise upon which the disaster movie, *The Day After Tomorrow (2004)* is based.

The absence of ice at the poles would also accelerate the increase in global temperature. This is because, if it were to melt, the ground would be much darker in colour and would no longer reflect so much of the sun's radiation back out into space. Freshly fallen snow, for example, absorbs only about 5% of the sun's radiation; for ice, the figure is between 10% and 40%. But the surface of the ocean can absorb up to 90% of incoming solar radiation which, over time, would dramatically increase the average global temperature.

1.

    a. Draw a graph to show rates of glacial melt between 2000 and 2018

    b. From your graph, make your own predictions about if/when all the ice will disappear from the Earth

2.

    a. Create a Mind Map to summarise what could happen if the rate at which the ice caps and glaciers melt increased rapidly.

3.

    a. How might mountain communities be affected by shrinking glaciers?

    b. How might they respond?

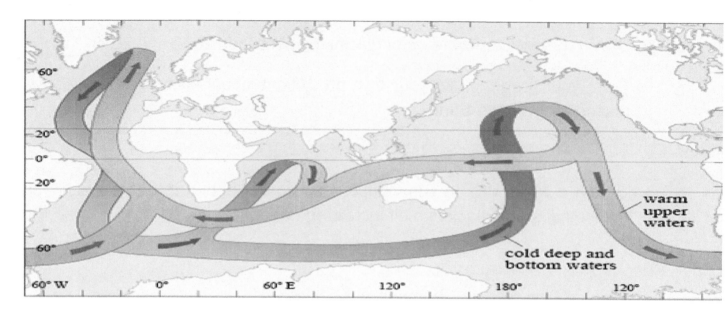

Background

If you have ever been on a foreign holiday, you know that, once your plane has landed, you go through immigration, then head for baggage reclaim. This is where your suitcases appear and travel around the arrival's hall on a giant conveyor belt until you finally recognise and rescue them. Far larger than this, in fact as large as the world itself, is the Great Ocean Conveyor Belt; but this doesn't move suitcases around, rather it shifts 2.0×10^7 (you might say 20 million) cubic metres of water across the oceans every single second. It is the earth's natural heat pump and its air conditioning system all rolled into one. The above diagram shows how it works.

Imagine, now, that the airport conveyor belt stopped running at a constant speed. Perhaps it slowed for a few moments, then suddenly sped up again or even stopped completely. People would either never get their suitcases back or they would have to frantically chase their luggage around. If the Great Ocean Conveyor Belt (GOCB) started playing up, however, things could get much worse.

How is it supposed to work?

Five currents make up the GOCB, the North and South Atlantic, North and South Pacific and the Indian Current. Wind, gravity, and water density move these vast quantities of water around. At the **equator**, the wind tugs on the ocean's surface and the **Coriolis Effect** causes the wind to spin, dragging the water towards the North and South Poles. When the water reaches colder latitudes, it cools down and sinks. One place where this happens is The Chimneys, which is a vast waterfall beneath the North Atlantic Ocean where columns 15 kilometres wide and 4 kilometres high 'recycle' the water, dragging it down to the ocean floor to begin its journey back down south. This constant movement of water moderates the climate of America's east coast and stops the weather in Western Europe from getting either too hot or too cold.

What is going wrong, then?

All this used to be predictable but, since routine monitoring began in 2004, certain currents have misbehaved. In the tropics, for example, the increase in global temperatures has caused them to speed up. This is because higher temperatures have made it windier and increased the size of waves in the open ocean. At higher latitudes, however, they have slowed down, perhaps by as much as 15% since 1950 in the case of the North Atlantic Drift. Scientists believe that this has something to do with the fresh water that is pouring off the ice caps in Greenland and Antarctica. This is diluting the ocean, making it less salty and less dense. This means it will not sink as easily as it used to and may, one day, not be 'recycled' at all. All this speeding up and slowing down also creates bottlenecks, rather like what happens on the motorway when cars insist on travelling at different speeds.

Can we be sure?

As we are only just starting to take an interest in these things, we do not yet have enough direct evidence to prove that there is a problem. However, it is possible to know what types of environments existed in the oceans long ago by examining deep-sea corals, analysing sediment on the ocean floor, and looking at ice cores and tree rings.

What could the effects be?

Changing ocean currents could cause all kinds of complications. To begin with, water would stack up along the eastern seaboard of the United States. This would cause the sea level to rise. It would also mean that the water spent longer in the tropics, where there would be more opportunity for it to warm up and fuel more tropical storms and hurricanes in a larger area of the Atlantic. Without the supply of warm water from the Caribbean, the temperature in much of Europe could fall by anything between 5 and 10°C. This would mean, for example, that the UK would get much more snow than it

does now and winter temperatures could remain below 0°C for lengthy periods, which would cause all kinds of problems relating to heating and transport. There would also be a serious impact on the fishing industry as, with the changing temperatures in the oceans, fish would either not thrive in such great numbers or would leave traditional fishing grounds, leaving many coastal communities without a livelihood. Shipping lanes could become crammed with icebergs that broke away from Greenland and floated off on erratic courses across the North Atlantic. This would cause havoc for cargo ships, which would be delayed by having to alter their course constantly to avoid them, adding to the economic impact of this environmental disaster. Erratic ocean currents could also cause rainfall patterns to change significantly so that there would be even less rainfall in Africa and some parts of Northern Europe than there is now.

Can anything be done?

While people have had some success managing the flow of water on the land, trying to manage the movement of water across the oceans would be almost impossible. One could, possibly, imagine a situation where we harvested vast amounts of salt from salt flats in the desert and dumped them in the North Atlantic to induce the weakening **maelstrom** that dragged the water back down into the deep ocean. More sensibly, we can redouble our efforts to reduce our emissions of **greenhouse gases**. In this way, we may be able to avoid warming the world up to an extent where these giant conveyor belts go out of control.

In what ways do we, living in Western Europe, benefit from the North Atlantic Drift? What might be the consequences of it breaking down?

1. The film The Day after Tomorrow is built on the premise that there could be a calamitous drop in temperature if the North Atlantic Current stops working.

    a. Watch the film.

    b. Do you think such a scenario is possible?

2. The film Finding Nemo features the turtles, Crush and Squirt, swimming in the East Australian current. Find out where this is. Is it depicted accurately in the film?

Background

On Wednesday 14 July 2021, a state of emergency was declared in Hagen, in the west of Germany as the River Volme rose to a level not normally seen more than four times in a single century. It burst its banks, one of many rivers in the Rhine Basin that did so, killing at least 58 people in the process. Then, barely a week later, the province of Henan in China was struck. 500 people had to be rescued from a flooded subway while the floodwaters also overwhelmed dams and caused landslides.

A problem that will not go away

These are just two examples from the summer of 2021 which further strengthen the argument that flooding over the coming decades is going to get worse. In the UK alone, it has put £200 billion of assets, including possessions, businesses and over 1.5 million properties at risk. In the winter of 2015/6, when the highest amount of rain to fall in a 24-hour period was recorded in the Lake District (341.4mm at Honister Pass), three rivers, the Eden, Tyne, and Lune, were discharging enough water to fill the Royal Albert Hall in under one minute. This is not a battle that people are likely to win. Scientists are more and more convinced that rainfall patterns are changing around the world.

Although we are heading towards a situation when there are likely to be fewer rainy days, there has been a 17% increase in extremely wet days (defined as days when the amount of rain reaches or exceeds the 95th percentile) from 1990 to 2020. High-intensity rainfall events and stronger storms are only going to occur more frequently in a warming world.

Protection, then prevention

There is little that can be done about this in the short to medium term. There has been too much human activity on flood plains for us to be able to turn back the clock overnight. The emphasis, for the time being, must be on protection as there are ways in which we can adjust to a wetter world. First, there is floodplain zoning. This is when we think about how we use the land that is most likely to flood and choose to build our homes, services (e.g., shops, schools, and hospitals) and important **infrastructure** (e.g., main roads and railway lines) on higher ground while leaving the lower ground to **agriculture** and recreation. We can also be better prepared for approaching storms through closer monitoring of the weather and of river systems, by setting up improved warning systems in areas that are likely to flood and by giving support to those affected by the rising waters. People can also be taught how to respond to the threat of flooding, for example by preparing flood plans for their homes and businesses. This will allow them to take decisive and effective action when the rivers rise. Dams, diversions, and barriers of all kinds, both permanent and temporary, can also be used to prevent floodwater from getting into homes and businesses.

Ultimately, however, putting up a fight against a wetter world is not a good use of our time or our money. What is more, rivers that are allowed to behave normally rather than being pinned back by dams and forced into straighter, channels with nothing living in them will eventually start to manage themselves far better than any human ever did. They will also provide a much wider variety of **habitat**s for birds, fish and amphibians than when people used to interfere with them.

We can work with nature to manage our river systems in many ways, although few will provide the quick fix solution that is achieved, at least briefly, by building bigger dams and digging deeper drains. One way is to slow down the flow of water in upland areas. This can be achieved over time by planting trees that both intercept rainfall and draw the water out of the ground and back into the atmosphere before it even reaches the rivers. Allowing vegetation to grow again in river channels and building natural dams out of wood debris might seem counterintuitive, that is, it goes against what seems to make sense. Yet if water can be delayed higher up in the valley for longer then it avoids a sudden 'crush' like the one that you often see at the entrance to a railway or tube station when everyone leaves a football match or a rock concert at the same time. Restoring rivers to their natural courses means that they can hold more water than when people redesigned them as high-speed routes to the sea. Certain parts of the floodplain can also be set aside upstream of towns and villages to contain the excess water at times when rainfall is high rather than letting it wash through people's homes. Changes in agricultural practices, such as farming less intensively, planting hedgerows, and changing the grazing habits of livestock can also help to slow down the rate at which rainwater passes through a drainage basin.

1. The River Derwent rises in the Lake District and flows through Cockermouth into the Irish Sea at Whitehaven. This chart gives its highest discharge for each year at five-yearly intervals from 1980 to 2010

Year	1980	1985	1990	1995	2000	2005	2010
Peak Flow in m3/sec	201	201	167	225	230	294	700

   a. Present the data in a suitable format, either on paper or using ICT.

   b. Describe the changes in the river's behaviour during this time.

   c. "The 2010 Floods in Cumbria were nothing more than a freak of nature". Do some research into these events. To what extent do you agree?

8.4 What if ... we stopped looking for Nemo?

Background

When Disney released the film *Finding Nemo* in 2003, millions of children and adults were captivated by its portrayal of the Great Barrier Reef with its crystal-clear waters and its amazing **biodiversity**. Yet almost twenty years later, almost half the reefs that existed when the film was made have been lost with some scientists even suggesting that we could be down to just 10% of the healthy reefs that existed in 2000 by the time we get to 2050.

Why are coral reefs so important?

Healthy coral reefs are of enormous benefit to us. They provide **habitat** as well as feeding, spawning and nursery grounds for over a million different aquatic species, provide food and recreation opportunities for people and are the source of many new medicines. The plankton that thrives there produces oxygen for us to breathe and reefs also afford some protection for coastal **infrastructure** when tropical storms come ashore, so limiting the damage that might otherwise be done to homes, harbours, and businesses.

What is going wrong?

Coral reefs are being damaged at an alarming rate. Part of the reason is the natural variation in global temperatures which cause the oceans to become slightly warmer when climate phenomena such as El Nino occur. In 2016, for example, water temperatures in the **equator**ial Pacific rose by over 2°C which is twice the increase that is required to trigger a bleaching event as irritated corals expel the algae that give them their vibrant colours.

People, however, are only making the situation worse. One of the most serious culprits is the fishing industry. When the reefs are overfished, their fine ecological balance is upset and fishing using dynamite (an explosive) and cyanide (a poison) scares off the fish that it doesn't kill. It also destroys the coral and muddies the water with sediments that block out the light. This is also what happens when **dredging** happens, for example to maintain access to marinas. There is also the global aquarium trade to consider. With as many as two million people worldwide keeping marine fish as a hobby, there is a growing demand for exotic fish. Many of these are taken directly from the open ocean and poor husbandry causes many fatalities. Then, there is the effect of tourism. Direct damage is done to the reefs when careless divers and swimmers touch living coral as well as when they drop their anchors on it. There is also the increased amount of sewage that tourism creates to consider. This floods the ocean with unwanted nutrients, causing algae to grow and block out the light on which the coral depends for survival.

What can be done about it?

The loss of healthy coral from the reefs can, however, be reversed. And it is not only those who live near them that have a role to play. We can all make greener choices when it comes to transport. Deciding to walk or cycle any distance under three miles, for example, would make a significant impact. This is because it would stop the ocean from becoming too acidic as it will reduce the amount of CO_2 that short car journeys pump out into the atmosphere unnecessarily. We can also choose to use sunscreen which does not contain harmful chemicals that pollute the water. Furthermore, by disposing of our rubbish responsibly so that what we throw away doesn't end up in the oceans, we can reduce the amount of plastic that ends up there.

Those that live in the vicinity of coral reefs can take additional action. Some scientists, for example, have recently started coral gardening. This is when healthy coral is taken from one place where it is thriving to another place where the plants have died. This used to be incredibly time-consuming but new technologies now allow as many as 200 pieces of coral to be transplanted in a single dive so that large areas of damaged coral can now be brought back to life in a relatively short space of time. Doing this has also provided work during the recent COVID lockdown for those who would otherwise have relied upon tourism for an income.

Other strategies have included the removal of invasive predators from the reefs, such as the Crown of Thorns Starfish. This marine invertebrate can decimate a reef in a very short space of time by feeding on the coral. Given the right conditions, they can reach plague proportions as they have only one predator, the Giant Triton Snail, that does not exist in large enough numbers to keep the starfish population under control. On another front, researchers are looking to the Red Sea to develop heat-resistant varieties of coral as well as, bizarrely, using sound recordings made in areas where coral is thriving to entice fish to return to damaged parts of the reef that they had previously abandoned.

In areas local to the reefs, the public can also get involved by preventing damage to the coral, by helping to keep the oceans free from rubbish and by limiting runoff from the land that may contain unwanted chemicals. This could mean persuading tourists to dive more responsibly or cutting down on their own use of water through rainwater harvesting and green **infrastructure**. This might include planting rain gardens that intercept rainfall while also improving water quality or green roofs on which grass and other low-lying vegetation intercept the rain.

1. This graph shows how both the number and severity of coral bleaching events have increased since records began in the early 1980s (Source: Hughes, T. P. et al., Spatial and temporal patterns of mass bleaching of corals in the Anthropocene, Science, 2018)

Number of coral bleaching events, Pacific

The number of moderate (up to 30% of corals affected) and severe bleaching events (more than 30% corals) measured at 100 fixed global locations. Bleaching occurs when stressful conditions cause corals to expel their algal symbionts.

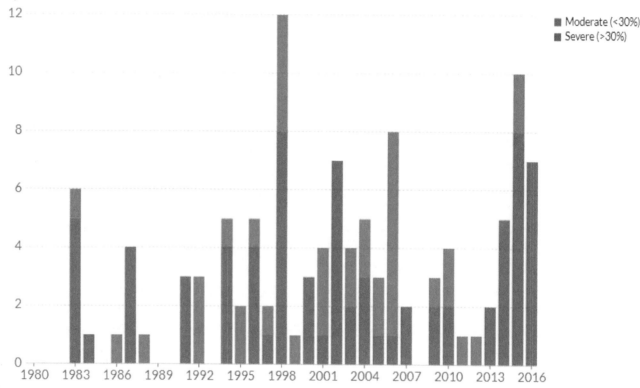

Legend: ■ Moderate (<30%) ■ Severe (>30%)

Source: Hughes, T. P., et al. (2018). Spatial and temporal patterns of mass bleaching of corals in the Anthropocene. Science.
OurWorldInData.org/biodiversity • CC BY

   a. In which years was the number of severe events greatest?

   b. What overall trends can you see?

2. Would you support a complete ban on the keeping of marine fish by hobbyists?

3. Most of us live a long way from any coral reef. What can we do to ensure their survival?

Background

It is impossible to know exactly how many kilometres of coastline there are on Earth. Estimates vary from just over 1.1 million to 1.63 million kilometres. Either way, it would take at least twenty years to walk their entire length at a fairly brisk pace. And you would only achieve that if you never stopped for a moment's rest.

Coasts are important places for people: they provide somewhere for them to live, trade, work, relax, find food and make money. They can also be very attractive. After all, who can resist the view from a spacious property overlooking a sun kissed waterfront? All of this helps to explain why around 40% of the world's population, or just over 3 billion people, live within 100km of the coast. They are also home to some of the most productive **ecosystems** on earth. Each square metre of swamp or marshland, for example, generates over 8000

kcal of energy in a year, which is the same as 35 standard-sized Mars bars. Perhaps this helps to explain why Shrek was so overweight!

Our attitude to the coast

We seem to have a love-hate relationship with the coast. Although it is so valuable to us, we treat much of it very badly. We build oil refineries and chemical plants along our coastlines and on our estuaries; we discharge all manner of waste into the sea, then dredge the seabed to replenish our shrinking beaches with sand and to keep our ports and harbours open. All of this stirs up sediments already polluted with sewage, discarded plastic and **agricultural runoff.** We catch vast quantities of fish almost indiscriminately and take back for our own use those parts of the coast which we deem to have little or no economic value. Here we do everything from growing rice to breeding fish and from dumping our rubbish to building new airports. We also put up ugly and, ultimately, futile defences against the power of the waves in the form of groins, rock armour and concrete sea walls, and succeed only in moving the problem a few miles up or down the coast.

Mangrove Forests

However, left to their own devices, coastal environments are remarkably good at looking after both themselves and the human population that depends on them. Until recently, mangrove forests, for example, have been seen as relatively useless environments and have been cut down to provide space for fish farms and paddy fields to feed Asia's ever-growing population. This may have provided increased food security in the short term. However, now that the forests have vanished, the coastline is much more exposed to being attacked by increasingly violent tropical storms. Neither is there the supply of wood that once provided coastal communities with timber for building and wood for fuel. The marine **habitat**s that used to support all manner of aquatic life are now decimated as the forest no longer absorbs the excess nutrients from runoff, nor does it trap the sediments which helped to keep the water clear and free from impurities.

Lately, however, attempts have been made to replant mangrove forests all over the world. But replicating the conditions under which they thrive has proved challenging and has turned out to involve more than simply planting new seedlings where the forest once was. For example, of the 3 million seedlings planted in The Philippines by the World Bank between 1984 and 1992, only half a million survived until 1996. And, even where they have survived, the emerging **habitat**s were not as rich and the communities not as **biodiverse** as the original ones because they consisted of just a single species of tree. A different approach, however, which involved clearing away much of the mud that had choked the coastline and allowing the tide to flow freely again, soon saw the mangroves re-establish themselves as the water brought seeds in from elsewhere. As Robin Lewis, the project leader, explained, "There wasn't a single mangrove planted in the whole project. Mother Nature can do such a great job of repairing herself if you give her the opportunity."

Salt marshes

At more temperate latitudes, which are places that are further from the **equator**, salt marshes do a similar job to the one done by mangroves in warmer climates. Land that was once reclaimed from the coast for agricultural purposes, however, is now being allowed to flood again with the ebb and flow of the tides. The sediments that accumulate because of this mean that as well as providing a natural barrier between the land and the sea the salt marshes will once again attract birds and marine life, purify the water and absorb CO_2. They will also continue to provide people with food and raw materials, to help to promote tourism and provide a place for recreation and scientific research

8.5 Things to do

1. In what ways do people abuse coastal environments?

2. Why is the restoration of coastal ecosystems such as salt marshes and mangrove forests…

   a. so important?

   b. so complicated?

3. To what extent is it acceptable to manage the coast in order to protect our economic interests?

4. "The coast can protect itself, so we should stop interfering." Do you agree?

Background

Everyone has the right to a proper education. This much was made clear in the Millennium Development Goals that were set out in September 2020 by the United Nations. In recent years there has been considerable progress towards this goal. For example, between 2000 and 2015, the percentage of children who are on roll at a primary school has increased from 83% to 91%. There has also been an improvement in the percentage of young people aged 15-24 who can read and write from 83% in 1990 to 91% in 2015.

And yet the picture is not all good. In 2020, 263 million children are still not attending school, a further 330 million are turning up, but learning nothing and 617 million are learning so little that they do not meet basic standards in Maths and Literacy. This is true of around 85% of all children in Sub-Saharan Africa. And, even in North America and Europe, 16% of all children fail to make the grade. Time spent actually l

learning can also be limited by a lack of teachers, who may not turn up because they are ill and/or have not been paid or by a shortage of resources.

Why go to school?

Education is empowering. First, it reduces **poverty** because it gives people the skills they need to do work which, in turn, will provide them with a wage to maintain a decent **standard of living**. Research suggests that for every year of schooling completed, a person's earnings potential increases by 10%. It also improves health as people learn to look after themselves and others; it promotes **democracy** and makes people aware of issues of **sustainability**. This means that they know what they can do to give the planet a chance at a better future. If the problem is not addressed urgently then the current generation of young people, the largest that the world has ever known, will be condemned to lives without purpose in which they persistently suffer from ill health and are caught up in political unrest and personal insecurity.

What's stopping people from learning?

There are all kinds of barriers to providing a decent education for all, one of which is the cost. In the rich nations of the world, we have become so used to school being both free and compulsory that we forget that others must pay for their education. Those who live in **poverty**, which is defined as having less than $1.90 (about £1.34 in July 2021) cannot afford even the meagre fees that have to be charged for tuition and resources in those parts of the world where the government makes little or no provision. Others, some say as many as 154 million, are kept from attending school by emergencies and disasters. For example, because of the ongoing civil war in Syria, up to 6,000 schools are closed indefinitely. On top of this, there is pressure on young people to work. Estimates suggest that there may be up to 169 million child labourers globally. Girls, who are still seen in many cultures as not as deserving of an education as boys, are many more times likely to drop out of school than boys when they are forced to marry and stay at home, some before they even become teenagers. Disability is also an obstacle to education with many millions not attending, either because they cannot physically get into the buildings or access teaching materials.

What is needed?

It is estimated that reaching the goal of delivering universal primary education will cost $3.5 trillion. Much of this will need to be invested in building classrooms that are fit for purpose, in bringing teachers up to standard, many of whom are barely trained at all, and in improving access to schools. Governments will need to raise taxes so that there is no upfront cost, and the disabled will need appropriate teaching spaces and facilities as well as suitable resources (e.g., wheelchairs for the physically impaired, books in Braille for the blind). Another problem that we can easily forget about is that there is often no safe way of getting to school for some children. Extreme weather, wild animals, even other people who object to them being taught can stand in their way. For example, in April 2014, over 250 Christian girls aged 16-18 were kidnapped from a boarding school in northern Nigeria. It is alleged that they were then made to convert to Islam married off to their captors and forced into sexual and domestic slavery. Few have since been rescued. There is, therefore, an urgent need to provide safer ways of getting to school for those living in remote, isolated, and politically unstable places. This could be as simple as providing a bus service or giving pupils bicycles so that they can travel further to school. Another alternative is to develop the technology to allow more people can learn without leaving their homes or to train up older students so that they can mentor younger pupils locally rather than requiring them to travel long distances to go on learning.

Things to do

1. This table shows the percentage of students reaching the most basic standards of education in five different countries in 2000 and 2015

	Norway	United Kingdom	Tunisia	China	Poland
2000	89%	90%	77%	95%	81%
2015	95%	89%	55%	92%	92%

   a. Present this data in a suitable format

   b. What might explain the very different fortunes of these five countries?

2. The text identifies five key barriers to education.

   a. Rank them from most to least problematic.

   b. Explain how you might go about overcoming one of the obstacles you have identified.

3. Turning up but learning nothing.

   a. To what extent is this a problem in schools around the world?

   b. Whose fault is it? Are the same people to blame in LICs as they are in HICs?

Background

As the world has become intricately connected in a process known as **globalisation**, some companies have become wealthier and more influential than entire countries. Taking advantage of the wealth of resources and talent all over the globe, they have become so huge that it would be unthinkable for them to fail. McDonalds is one such transnational corporation. With over 37,000 restaurants in well over half the countries in the world, it serves around 69,000,000 customers daily which is almost 1% of the global population. In the USA alone, 85 million people eat in its restaurants every day. It also employs 1.7 million people globally and still has ambitious plans for expanding further. In China over the next three years, for example, it plans to open a new restaurant every day for the next three years.

If Ronald shut the doors ...

If McDonalds were to cease trading, there would be consequences for the environment, the economy and for society. The consequences for the environment would be the most significant. To begin with, it would spare 11 million beef cattle from slaughter, of which 5.5 million are destined for the US market alone. The average cow produces around 430 pounds (around 210 kg) of meat, of which a little less than half is ground to make mince. One cow therefore provides roughly 800 quarter pounders which, when consumed at the global rate of 75 burgers per second, means that the average cow keeps McDonalds in business for eleven seconds. Clearly all these cows being spared from the abattoir would be good news for vegetarians and, over time, would significantly reduce the demand to open up more of the rainforest to cattle ranching. This is something that McDonalds has made a commitment to but has yet to achieve as, while the forest is no longer cleared away for ranching, companies chop trees down to provide the space to grow the soya beans on which we feed both cattle and chickens. It would also mean less exploitation of debt slaves. These are people who are promised work in the forest but who are paid so little and charged so much for their food and transport that they are trapped there in a cycle of **poverty**. If a drive towards zero commercial **deforestation** by 2040 were to be successful, this would preserve **habitat**s and sustain **biodiversity**. After a time, there would also be a significant decline in emissions of methane which is a greenhouse gas that contributes to **global warming**. Another environmental benefit would be that large amounts of water that were once drunk by the cattle and used to grow their food would become available to irrigate crops destined for human consumption. From an environmental perspective, therefore, the disappearance of McDonalds would be a broadly positive thing.

From a socio-economic perspective, however, which is to say when it comes to the effects on people and money, the consequences would be more finely balanced. With a revenue of over $40 billion dollars every year, the disappearance of McDonalds would take a significant chunk out of Global Gross Domestic Product (GDP), equivalent to the wealth of some entire countries. This could slow down economic growth considerably. There would also be massive unemployment, chiefly in high-income countries (HICs). This would add considerably to the social security budget as and, possibly, lead to a rise in **poverty**, crime, and homelessness as hundreds of thousands of people all entered the job market at the same time with not enough employers to hire them. More positively, many people's diets might improve as they consume less sodium, fatty acids, and sugar. Thus, the cost of tackling health problems related to obesity, such as heart disease, strokes and certain cancers would reduce as diets improved. People might also start cooking for themselves again, rejecting a culture of fast food with its excessive packaging and dubious ingredients for healthier options. Their food choices might also keep the distinct cultures of certain parts of the world alive as opposed to allowing them to be further eroded in a world in which almost everyone already drinks Coca Cola, wears Nike trainers and watches Disney movies. This could support their mental as well as their physical wellbeing as sharing a meal is one activity that is proven to hold families and communities together, far better than snacking on pizza while playing video games at your computer!

We would see another economic consequence of the disappearance of McDonalds on the High Street as its restaurants often occupy some of the most sought-after locations in city centres. Provided that landlords were realistic in terms of the rent that they charged any subsequent tenant, this could bring more diversity into our city centres, making them places people wanted to visit rather than to avoid.

So, the consequences of the sudden disappearance of McDonalds are not as clear-cut as one might imagine. The rainforest might breathe a sigh of relief for a time but the knock-on effects for the economy would be hard to manage. However, one thing is for certain: there will be no more pesky plastic toys taking up space in landfill sites.

1. From 2009 to 2021, the total household spend on fast food in the UK grew from £7.4 billion £11.2 billion per year.

   a. Assuming that the potential market is around 50 million people (if we forget about babies, vegetarians, and people on restricted diets)

      i.   What is the average spend per person on fast food?

      ii. What is the percentage increase in the amount spent between those years?

   b. 'The benefits of having access to plenty of cheap fast food, including takeaways and microwaveable meals outweighs the environmental costs.' Do you agree? Explain your answer.

2. How does being able to cook give you control over what you eat?

3. People who are obese are more of a burden on society than those who are starving. Knowing this to be true, what should our priorities be when trying to influence people's diets?

Background

In the film, *WALL-E,* life on Earth has become un**sustainable**. To allow time for recovery, the authorities send thousands of people off into outer space. There, they sit around idly while robots meet all their needs. It is a rather extreme scenario, but the idea of a leisure-based society, one in which there is no need for most people to work, is not new.

Throughout history, there has been a privileged class who have not needed to work to earn a living. Many of them have spent their time and money supporting the Arts, working for charities, or getting involved in politics. Lately, however, the possibility has arisen that there might be too little work for large numbers of people, especially in the Global North. Must we adjust to a lifestyle in which work no longer dominates our lives?

The idea of leisure

People first thought life might eventually become one long holiday in the 1920s. However, nobody took the idea seriously until the middle of the 20th century. Experts suggested then that the reduction in working hours that had taken place since the Second

World War might continue into the later part of the 20th century. An author called Dahl - not the one who wrote *Charlie and the Chocolate Factory* - thought that we would see shorter working weeks and longer holidays. He also predicted people would spend longer in education and retirement and that leisure would become an industry in its own right.

Could we all sit around doing nothing?

It might seem appealing to have no work to do at all. However, most people do not think it is possible and many dislike the idea, anyway. Even if computers controlled our lives and each of us had our own personal robot, some people would still have to work. After all, who is going to build the robots in the first place or program them? And who will perform other roles robots cannot do, such as make and enforce laws and teach future generations? A life without work would take away many people's sense of purpose and identity and leave them doubting their self-worth. So many conversations between strangers start, "What do you do for a living?" that not being able to answer could also be very embarrassing. "Me...? Erm, I do nothing." A life of doing nothing also seems unlikely for another reason, too. This is because **capitalism**, which is a way of life for many in the Global North, forbids it. It insists that we go on making loads of manufactured goods, convince others they need them, and then sell them. The choices that we make in our leisure time must, therefore, be ones that require other people to work... whether as lifeguards, leisure centre managers, personal coaches, or entertainers' onboard luxury cruise liners.

What might happen, then?

What could happen is a kind of 'turning upside down' of how society is organised. In the past, most people worked hard for a living and very few people could pass their time in idle luxury. In the future, assuming that much unskilled and semi-skilled can be done by robots, a few people will do a limited variety of very well-paid jobs while masses of people, who I will call the 'enforced idle' will need to find other things to do with their time.

This could cause quite a few problems including some conflict. Those who had to work would resent the large numbers of people who, through no fault of their own, had nothing to do. They would have to find constructive ways of using their time. Then they might be seen to contribute positively to society rather than as spongers who lived at the expense of others. The work-free masses would also have to contend with challenges to their mental and physical wellbeing to avoid problems such as anxiety and depression. It would also be a challenge for them to not get caught up in the vandalism, violence, alcoholism, and drug abuse that so easily entrap idle hands and minds.

Is there any hope?

An alternative future is possible. One in which those who do what we now call 'work' and those who occupy themselves in other ways are equals. It is not so foolish to ask to be paid a decent wage for what we now call 'leisure'. Today, as I write this, news has come through that Jack Grealish has been offered £100 million to kick a football around with a light blue jersey on for six years. So why should we not offer homemakers, carers, and artists the same opportunity?

Achieving this goal will be challenging, and there will be wide-ranging implications. Mass education, for example, which was designed in the mid-nineteenth century to fill the factory floor, would have to be replaced with tailored learning, where people were taught on a need-to-know basis rather than being fed the same diet of knowledge and skills. We will have to devise more productive ways of using our downtime and reject the idea that people should only have money if they have done what we now regard as work. People will have to be encouraged to learn new skills, take on new hobbies and invest time in their relationships in their non-working time as well as prioritising their health. This is already happening and, with the creation of National Parks, the growth of leisure centres, increasing numbers of personal trainers, gyms and exercise classes, everyone might be able to make good use of whatever spare time they are fortunate enough to enjoy.

9.3 Things to do

1. The chart below shows how the number of hours worked in a year by the average employee has changed for several selected countries (Source: Our World in Data)

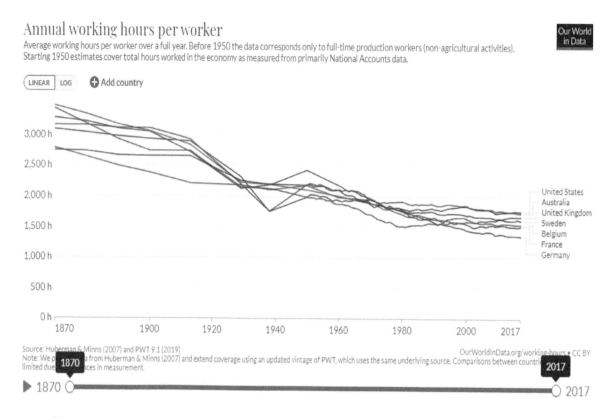

Annual working hours per worker
Average working hours per worker over a full year. Before 1950 the data corresponds only to full-time production workers (non-agricultural activities). Starting 1950 estimates cover total hours worked in the economy as measured from primarily National Accounts data.

LINEAR LOG ⊕ Add country

United States
Australia
United Kingdom
Sweden
Belgium
France
Germany

Source: Huberman & Minns (2007) and PWT 9.1 (2019)
OurWorldInData.org/working-hours • CC BY
Note: We p____ from Huberman & Minns (2007) and extend coverage using an updated vintage of PWT, which uses the same underlying source. Comparisons between countri___
limited due ___ ces in measurement.

▶ 1870 ○――――――――――――――――――――――――○ 2017

a. Can you

   i. Describe the pattern that is shown.

   ii. Explain the fall from around 3000 hours a year in 1900 to around 2000 hours a year in 1940?

   iii. Explain the 'spike' in Germany in the 1940s?

b. The 21st century has seen the number of hours worked by the average person stagnate at around 1500 hours per year. Why do you think this is?

2. Given that many jobs might become automated within the next generation, what careers advice would you give to young people today?

Background

Development is one of the main goals of every country in the world. The trouble is, we don't seem able to agree on what it is. People have a whole variety of ways of measuring it, and what looks like progress if we use one set of statistics looks like anything but if we choose another. Different views on what counts as progress and how it should be measured also have a significant impact on how governments run their countries and relate to the rest of the world. Does money make the world go around, as some people would have us believe, or is there more to it than that?

Way, way back many centuries ago

It was only fifty years ago or so that Gross Domestic Product, or GDP, per person was the only thing that really mattered. You simply added up the total value of all a country's goods and services and divided it by the population and there was your answer. This

wasn't terribly helpful for all kinds of reasons. First, it didn't tell us anything about how the money was shared out; was it equally distributed or did just a few people control a large share of it? Did a small group of well-off people drive around in limousines and dine in luxury every evening while the majority starved and couldn't afford a bicycle? There was no way of knowing. It also meant that countries felt compelled to make money, whatever the cost, so they became much less interested in people's welfare or the state of the environment.

A step in the right direction

A more helpful way of measuring progress was put forward by Mahbub ul Haq and his colleague Amartya Sen in 1990. They suggested that three further things should be used to determine a country's level of development: life expectancy at birth, average years of schooling and expected years of schooling. They created a scale from 0.0 to

1.0, where any score <0.6 suggested limited development and any score over 0.8 indicated a highly developed country. This was a broader measure of a country's success but there were still some things that had been forgotten about. This is the human development index.

A clearer picture altogether

Since 1990, people who study development have refined their definitions of what counts as progress and how it should be measured even further. One idea was for a social progress index which would look at how well the country met basic human needs (e.g., for food, shelter and security), whether they had laid the 'foundations for wellbeing' (e.g. provided appropriate health care and clean water for everyone) and whether people had the opportunity to lead fulfilling lives (e.g. by working or having the chance to make a contribution to society in another way). Scoring countries on a scale from 0 to 100, Norway was top of the list with 92.7 and South Sudan at the bottom, with only 31.06.

There was also the Inclusive Development Index (IDI), launched more recently in 2018. This aimed to reflect an even greater number of aspects of quality of life which were grouped under three headings: growth and development, inclusion, and **sustainability** and **intergenerational equity**. The last of these is, admittedly, a bit of a mouthful but is essentially about whether a particular generation chooses to meet its own needs without stuffing things up for their grandchildren or just takes what they want without thinking about the consequences. The IDI looks, for example, at how widespread **poverty** is in the country, how much money the

government has borrowed, the size of the average **carbon footprint** and at how serious a problem pollution is there. It also considers how quickly finite resources are being used up.

Perhaps the most innovative approach to the question of how progress should be measured, however, was that of the government of a tiny mountainous state in the Himalayas, Bhutan. As far back as the eighteenth century, long before the Human Development Index or the Inclusive Development Index were even thought of, the kingdom's first legal code stated that "if the government cannot create happiness for its people, there is no purpose for the government." Then, in the 1970s, King Jigme took this idea further. Now Gross National Happiness (GNH) is at the centre of all decision making in the kingdom. Psychological well-being, **standard of living**, good governance, health, community vitality, cultural diversity, time use, and ecological resilience now must all be considered by law, when making new legislation.

Despite interest in the idea of GNH from many parts of the world, however, Bhutan remains a very poor country. Still largely dependent upon **agriculture** for its wealth and well-being, it is already suffering from more extreme weather events which wash away its soils and melt its **glacier**s. It ranked 121st in the world on the inclusive development index (the UK was 5th), 129th in the world for HDI (the UK was 13th) and had a GDP per capita of $3,122 whereas the UK's is $41,855. However good its ideas are in theory, the aspects of life that the concept of GNH is designed to measure may deteriorate before there is much time to address them.

1. This graph (Source: Researchgate) shows the relationship between self-reported happiness and GDP.

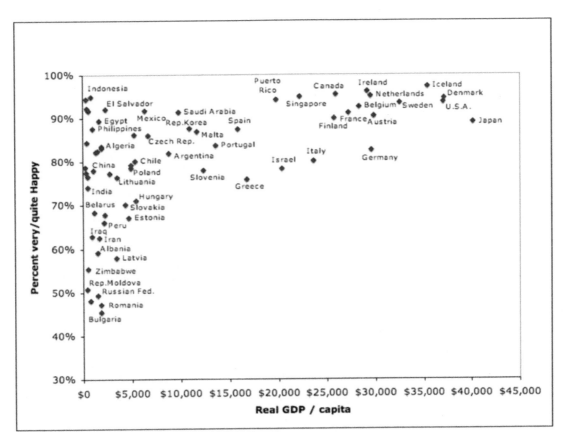

a. What does it tell us about the link between wealth and happiness (if there is one)?

b. "The poor can still be perfectly happy." What evidence is there from this graph that this is true?

c. Identify the countries that are relatively rich and yet relatively miserable. What do they have in common?

2. How have ways of measuring human development become more accurate over the years?

3. Design your own tool for working out how advanced a country is. What kinds of statistics would you include/leave out? How might it help governments make decisions about the future?

Glossary

agricultural runoff	water that washes off fields used for farming
agriculture	farming
amenity	a service or facility made available to the public, e.g. a swimming pool, a park, or a library
aquifer	a rock that holds water
artificial intelligence	computer systems that can do what humans do
biodiversity	the variety of living things
biofuel	a fuel that is obtained from plants
caldera	a crater left when a volcano collapses
capitalism	a system in which making things and money is important
carbon budget	a limit on the volume of **greenhouse gases** that a person or country can emit
carbon emission	the release of carbon dioxide, methane, and carbon monoxide into the atmosphere
carbon footprint	the amount of carbon dioxide released into the atmosphere because of the activities of a particular individual, organization, or community.
carbon-neutral	having no overall effect on carbon emissions
climate change	changes to the patterns that weather follows around the world
clone town	a town that looks much like any other, e.g., full of chain stores
consumerism	a system in which people are encouraged to buy and use as many products and services as possible
convection	the movement of heat
Coriolis effect	the deflection of wind and ocean currents caused by the spinning of the earth
counterurbanisation	the process by which people leave towns and cities and go to live in rural areas
crude oil	a fossil fuel made of the remains of dead marine creatures

cultural erosion	the loss of individual beliefs, values, and traditions
deforestation	the removal of trees
delta	an area found at the mouth of a river where it splits into many channels, called distributaries
democracy	a system of government in which, in theory at least, every individual gets a say
dependency ratio	the relationship between the number of people who can work as opposed to those who cannot
desalination	the removal of salt
desertification	the process by which fertile land becomes desert, typically because of drought, deforestation, or inappropriate agriculture.
dredging	removing sediment from the bottom of a river or sea
drought	the absence of rain over an extended period
earth killers	meteorites so large as to be capable of ending civilisation
ecosystem	a community of living and non-living things
equator	the line of zero degrees latitude
eradicating	getting rid of
evaporation	turning from a liquid into a gas
extremist	a person who actively promotes values and beliefs that are not typical of the majority, often violently
fertiliser	something applied to the soil to make it more productive; can be organic or chemical
fertility rate	the average number of live children born to each woman who survives her child-bearing years
floodplain	the area a river floods when it bursts its banks
food chain	a diagram which shows the connections between producers and consumers in an ecosystem
food waste	anything that is edible but gets thrown away instead
fossil fuel	any fuel derived from plant or animal matter
genetic mutation	the alteration of the genes of a plant or animal usually to improve its performance
geothermal	to do with heat from the earth
gerontology	the study of the elderly and their particular problems

glacier	a river of ice
global warming	a gradual increase in the overall temperature of the earth's atmosphere
globalisation	the process by which the world is increasingly interconnected
greenhouse gases	those gases which act as an insulating layer around the earth, including CO_2, methane and water vapour
groundwater	water that flows through soil and rock as opposed to over the ground
habitat	a place where something lives
hectare	a measurement of area equal to $10,000m^2$
HIC	High Income Country
housing density	the number of properties built in any given area
infant mortality	the number of children per thousand born live who die before their first birthday
infertile	not useful for growing anything
infiltration	the process by which rainwater soaks into the ground
infrastructure	the buildings, roads, power supplies and other utilities that settlements need to function
intergenerational equity	making things fair for all age groups
LIC	Low Income Country
light pollution	light that shines where it is not wanted or needed
low-carbon technology	any process that helps to reduce carbon emissions
maelstrom	a whirlwind
malnourishment	when you do not get enough of the right things to eat
mantle	the layer of semi-molten rock directly below the earth's crust
megacity	a city with over ten million inhabitants
micronutrients	nutrients that exist in very small amounts
microplastics	tiny fragments of plastic, often too small to be seen
mitigation	attempts to lessen the impact of something
multiplier effect	when one economic benefit leads to another

omnivores	creatures that eat both plants and animals
pesticides	chemicals used to kill unwanted insects
poverty	having insufficient money to take your place in society
refugee	a person who has escaped from danger
replacement rate	the average number of babies that must be born to each woman if the population is not to decline
reservoir	a body of water that collects behind a dam
rural-urban fringe	the zone where town and countryside meet
sky glow	the yellow-orange hue that shines around towns and cities because of dust and water vapour in the air
standard of living	the degree of wealth and material comfort available to a person or community
supervolcano	a volcano capable of ejecting ten thousand cubic kilometres of rock and ash or more
sustainable	capable of satisfying present needs without negatively affecting future needs
sweatshop	a factory where people work in poor conditions
synthetic fibres	material from which clothes are made that is not natural, e.g., polyester
terrorist	a person who uses unlawful violence and intimidation, especially against civilians, in the pursuit of political aims
transpiration	when plants release water vapour into the atmosphere
urban heat island	the increase in temperature caused by a high density of people and buildings
urbanisation	the process by which greater numbers of people come to live in urban areas
wetland	an area near a river's estuary that floods with the incoming tide